Photo: Mary Hammonds

NEVILLE PEAT, a leading interpreter of nature, draws inspiration for his writing from the powerful landscapes and seascapes of southern New Zealand. He has written more than 20 books, including *Forever the Forest*, *The World of Albatrosses* and *The Falcon and the Lark*.

Three titles from his 'Wild' book series have been shortlisted for the Montana Book Awards with *Wild Dunedin* winning the Montana Natural Heritage Award in 1996.

While under contract to the Department of Conservation he wrote the successful nomination of the New Zealand Subantarctic Islands as a World Heritage Area in 1998. An Otago Regional Councillor, with a strong interest in sustainable development and conservation, Neville lives on Otago Peninsula with his wife Mary and daughter Sophie.

COASTING
The Sea Lion and the Lark

Neville Peat

Longacre Press

The author thanks Creative New Zealand for providing a project grant towards the completion of research and writing of this book. Published with the assistance of

This book is copyright. Apart from any fair dealing for the purpose of private study, research, criticism or review, as permitted under the Copyright Act, no part may be reproduced by any process without prior permission of Longacre Press and the author.

Neville Peat asserts his moral right to be identified as the author of this work.

© Neville Peat

ISBN 1 877135 57 7

First published by Longacre Press, 2001
9 Dowling Street, Dunedin, New Zealand

Book and cover design by Jenny Cooper
Maps drawn by Christine Buess
Printed by Brebner Print, Auckland, New Zealand

Contents

Preface 7

Maps 8

Beginnings 11

PART I The Mouth 19

PART II Enderby 61

PART III Going South 79

PART IV Going North 119

PART V Moturata 133

PART VI New Frontier 142

PART VII The Mouth Revisited 158

Ongoings 179

Acknowledgements 183

AT TAIERI MOUTH

Flax-pods unload their pollen
Above the steel-bright cauldron
Of Taieri, the old water-dragon
Sliding out from a stone gullet

Below the Maori-ground. Scrub horses
Come down at night to smash the fences

Of the whaler's children. Trypots have rusted
Leaving the oil of anger in the blood

Of those who live in two-roomed houses
Mending nets or watching from a window

The great south sky fill up with curdled snow.
Their cows eat kelp along the beaches.

The purple sailor drowned in thighboots
Drifting where the currents go

Cannot see the flame some girl has lighted
In a glass chimney, but in five days' time

With bladder-weed around his throat
Will ride the drunken breakers in.

JAMES K. BAXTER
1961

Preface

At Taieri Mouth, south of Dunedin, there is a new presence riding the breakers in. I want to describe it and define it. I want to try to understand it.

NEVILLE PEAT
Broad Bay
2001

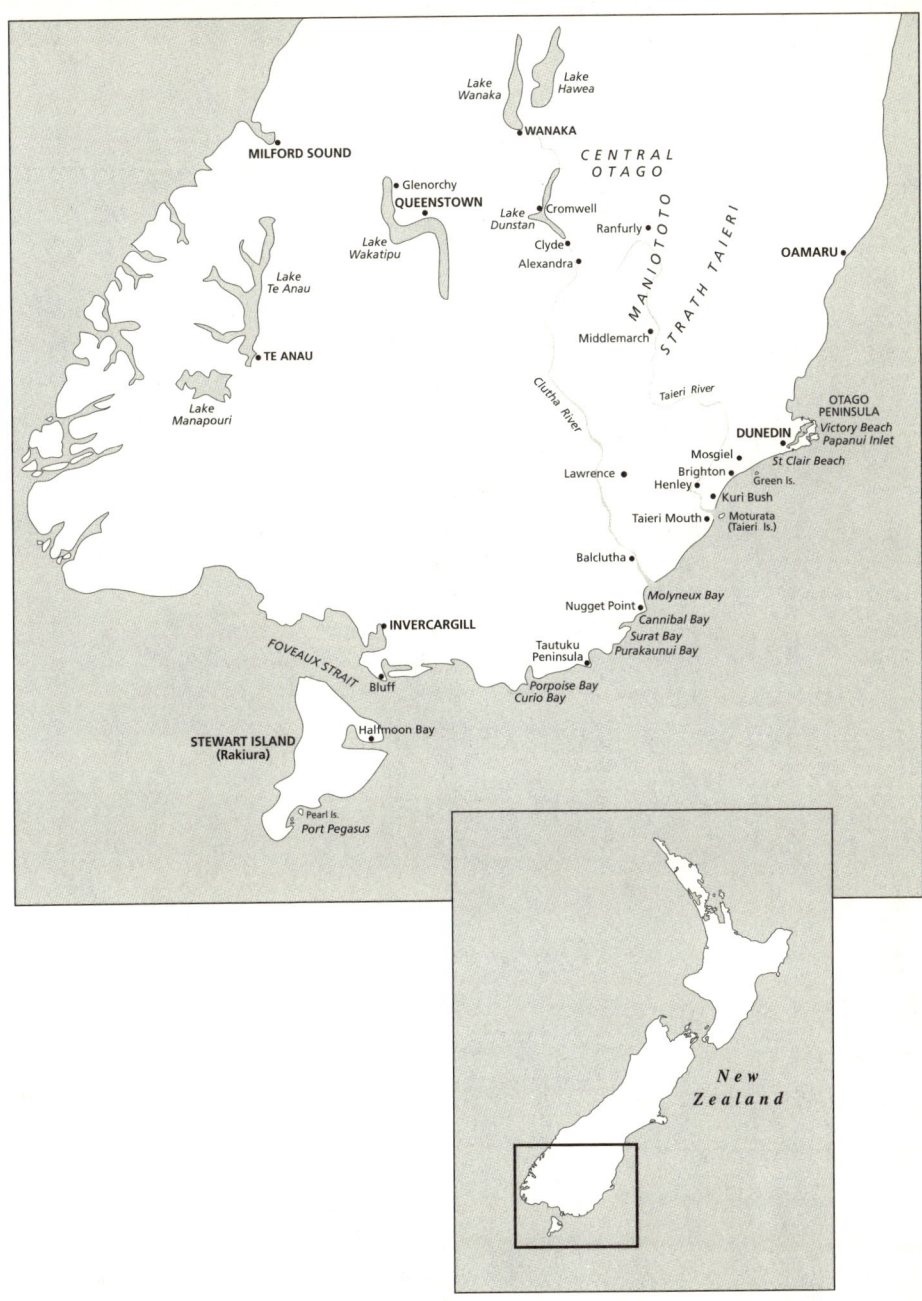

Beginnings

BIG ROCK CORNER, at Brighton, is a milestone on the road to Taieri Mouth. No, it is more than a milestone. It is a threshold. Approaching from the Dunedin side, you negotiate a U-turn around a bluff high above the crashing sea. The world seems to spin. You feel at the edge of somewhere special, and when the spinning is over it looks too good to be true. Immediately below, threatening to excite a vertigo attack, is Brighton Beach, hemmed in by cliffs on the near side and a river on the far side. No matter how many tiny figures are distributed on the beach, it always appears to be a private sort of place – a snug fit for the sea. Even lines of surf caress the sand. Beyond the quiet river is a giant billiard table – a footy field in reality, the Domain. Cliffs of crumbling clay and schist bedrock elevate the Domain above river and sea, a green tongue licking water that is effervescent and salty on one side, and dark, sluggish and brackish on the other. With no estuary to relax into before submitting to the sea, Brighton River moves sullenly and reluctantly to its destiny. Its mouth is nondescript, mostly a dribble of water crossing the sand and stained the colour of tea. Sometimes the sea closes the mouth completely – and the brew thickens.

The backdrop to the bay contains houses new, old and refurbished, the newer ones having been enticed by favourable council rates and a gorgeous outlook. Only a few holiday cottages remain where once they were cheek by jowl, a picture of summer bonhomie. Called cribs this far south in New Zealand, they used to be shuttered up for months on end awaiting a rush of blood known as the school holidays. The cribs speak of a time when petrol was cheap and society homogenous, and when you went to Brighton for a dip in the sea. Bikinis were just starting to make an impact. It was fashionable for the blokes to slick Brylcream through their hair. It kept their hair glossy, even after a dip.

This is where my coasting began. For a youngster growing up on the other side of the coastal hills at flat, featureless Mosgiel, a trip to Brighton was an adrenaline adventure. It was another country. Big Rock corner, the border, made my heart jump. It still does. Forty years on, I go back and kick the creamy-grey sand, suck in salt air tainted with rotting bull and bladder kelp – and cross a memory threshold. The 'fifties were full of endless summers. Bottler days. Corkers. Especially Saturdays. 'You could rely on it to be fine,' my mother would say, looking back. From Mosgiel, Brighton was two short bus rides away, and it added to the excitement to have to swap buses at Green Island.

My father, Ernie, never came on these trips. He coveted fresh water. Whenever we went to Brighton, he would head for the Taieri River or some other inland waterway with a fishing rod and a tin of worms dug up squirming from the garden for bait. I never saw him in bathing togs.

Yet, despite the fact that we went different directions, we shared an interest in the tides. If Dad intended fishing the tidal lower Taieri River around Henley he needed to know what the tide was doing at Taieri Mouth and how it would affect the feeding routines of trout and flounder. The Brighton expeditions were also tidally driven. We beach-goers had to coincide with low tide. We might stay at home otherwise. At Brighton, low tide exposed rock pools by the acre to the south of the surfing beach. The pools were fantasy worlds in miniature. And they were worlds apart, each uniquely designed, decorated and inhabited. Cockabullies ruled. We would pile on to the bus at Mosgiel with togs, towels, sunhats and sandwiches – and numerous jars with screwtop lids for catching the large-headed little fish. We started going fairly regularly to Brighton when I was six years old. Mum would take my younger brother, Russell, and I, and our similar-aged cobbers from over the road, Frankie and Nan Burrell – plains kids on a marine mission. The New Zealand Railways Bedford bus, whose dark-green vinyl seats would stick to the backs of our legs on a hot day, let us out at the bottom of the hill below the Big Rock. We usually had one thing on our minds. We would make straight for the rock pools after selecting a picnic spot at the edge of the marram grass backing the broad apron of sand. We would leave our food, clothes and other possessions there unguarded. Safe as houses, they were. Nothing ever went missing.

If the weather was uncommonly hot we might head for the surf first, but mostly we went hunting cockabullies in the hope of giving them a bus ride home. We also sought catseye shellfish with the passion of gemstone hunters, and loved watching their jade-green doors swing shut when they were plucked, squirting, from the pools.

A tide island protecting the main beach from southerly swells was the first island I ever stepped on. I have been intrigued by islands ever since. Flat and grassed on top, Barney's Island had a deep natural trench through it, dark at the bottom. We waded the channel if the tide was half in, or leapt across. My mother never ventured over. It added to the mystery of the place to be rid of our adult escort.

As the tide came in and the surf grew more boisterous, we might retreat to the river, where the water was tepid, if a trifle slimy. The river arced back to a single-lane wooden bridge with a footpath on the upstream side. We would lean over the rail and admire the comings and goings of canoes and rowboats that were for hire from a large well-stocked boatshed close by. I had just turned eight when, leaning over the guardrails one day, I asked my mother if I could take out a boat. Having never been in a boat in her life, she was probably startled by the idea but gave it a go anyway. We had a double canoe to start with and later graduated to a rowboat so that all the kids could come.

Before the summer was out we were exploring a fair way up the river. It was our Amazon. Tapir might thud warnings in the river-bank forest. We'd listen out for troops of squealing monkeys and deep-throated parrots in the canopy and scan the black unplumbed depths beneath the boat for water snakes and razor-toothed piranhas. When the jungle gave way upstream to cattle paddocks thick with docks and other weeds, the jungle fauna receded. A weir a mile or so from the village stopped progress altogether. Anyway, we had to get back. There was a deadline to meet, chalked up on a blackboard back at the boatshed.

Revisiting Brighton, I find most things are reduced in scale and somewhat demystified. The marram grass skirting Brighton Beach, once good for hide-and-seek, comes up to my knees now, and the cliffs around the Domain are not the towering challenges they once were. I remember the curtains of native iceplant, which provided handholds and footholds for young mountaineers. Down on the beach near the island, are the broken-down concrete walls of an open-air saltwater pool whose designers figured that high tides would replenish it. But the pool did not work in my boyhood and it still does not work. Sand has flooded it. Sand hoppers and scarabs enjoy the pool but it gets little use otherwise – someone's brainwave foiled by the shifting sands.

Bare feet have been warmed and massaged by the sands of Brighton for centuries. Moa hunters camped here 500 years or more ago. They left their marks, blackening the soil where they had cooking fires and leaving behind moa bones and mussel shells. They lived off land and sea. The moa, flightless ratite birds related to the kiwi but larger, were a staple, hunted not only locally but also on excursions into the semi-arid interior or to the great southern rainforests of the Catlins region. Moa supplemented what the sea had to offer. Of course, the sea itself offered plenty. When the tide was out, the table was all but laid.

Brighton has always been a wonderful place for a picnic. But these early people had more than a day's recreation in mind. When Julius von Haast passed here in 1879, he described Otokia Mouth as 'an ancient manufactory' from the moa-hunter era. He was talking about the manufacture of stone tools. He found chunks of volcanic basalt that had been roughly hammered into adze shape.

As a kid I never stumbled upon signs of ancient human endeavour in the crumbling cliffs or on the island. But then, I was not looking for them. Cockabullies, catseyes and other denizens of rock pools were fulfilment enough for me. Plus the surf and sand, of course.

And although I did not know it at the time, Brighton provided early inspiration for poet James K. Baxter, who went to primary school here 20 years earlier. Brighton was the centre of Baxter's life until he left secondary school. The sea, surf, shore, river, hills, bush and township presented images that would live on in his poems. To Baxter, Brighton would remain 'the home each sailor loves and runs away from'. By the time he died at the age of 46 in 1972, Baxter was barefoot and long-bearded, a prophet of sorts, living humbly by the Wanganui River, a long way from Brighton.

We all move on. Moa hunters camped at Brighton off and on. Judging by the bones they left here, some serious eating took place. Besides moa, fur seals were consumed. Possibly sea lions, too. A vertebra thought to be that of a sea lion was recovered from the cliff edge. If I had been confronted by a full-grown male sea lion on Brighton Beach 40 years ago I might have been scared off the place forever, fantasy world or not.

Yet sea lions have lured me back. I come not with the subsistence interest of a moa hunter but with a naturalist's sense of wonder and interest in processes, and a writer's eye for an angle. There is a good story here. The people who hunted moa – and hastened their extinction – also drove the sea lions from mainland New Zealand. It happened around 400 years ago. Archaeologists excavating kitchen remains at ancient camp and settlement sites report that sea lion bones disappear about then, everywhere. Through overhunting, the early people lost a supermarket supply of steak borne on flippers from the sea. But the tide has turned for sea lions. Towards the end of the 20th century, sea lions began reclaiming Otago's shores.

The focus of my attention is not so much Brighton as the mouth of the Taieri River, 20 kilometres further south. In years to come, when sea lions are once again widely if thinly distributed on mainland New Zealand – southern regions at least – Taieri Mouth will be hailed as a threshold. A pup was born here around Christmas 1993. It marked the return of a long-lost species.

Taieri Mouth was half a world away when I was a boy. I suppose I knew you could get there by driving along the coast but I never went. Brighton was the end of the line. Few buses travelled past Brighton, and electricity was also slow to move south. Today you can scoot through Brighton and reach Taieri Mouth by way of a slick ribbon of tarseal squeezed between the farmland and the sea. Small, chaste beaches are temptingly close. I feel like pausing at each one. I could leave a mark for the next tide to extinguish. But generally I push on. Taieri Mouth is an adventureland these days – and I have graduated from cockabullies.

PART I

The Mouth

ONE

ON THE DAY Britain handed back Hong Kong to the mainland Chinese, I encountered something curiously oriental at Taieri Mouth. Oriental cats. Siamese actually, a trio of purebreds. I have come to talk to their owner, George McIntosh, about whiskered carnivores with a big-cat name – sea lions. But as far as letting George and I discuss sea lions, the Siamese have other ideas.

'Come on now, Charlie,' George says as I step into his house overlooking the dunes on the northern side of the river mouth. 'Let our visitor have that comfortable chair, there's a good boy.' The instruction is delivered with a measure of tact. I realise then George is more a caregiver than an owner of these cats.

'He'll hang around, you watch,' he says. 'Charlie doesn't much like sharing me.' And so Charlie, who has another name, Aldebaran, the name of a star, a name more in keeping with his breeding – Charlie butts in from time to time for no other reason, I guess, than that he is a bit put out by the visitor. He keeps interrupting us with loud, arresting Siamesespeak and haughty body language. Perhaps, too, on this dull still winter's day, with nothing much moving inside or out except for the sea nearby curling and crashing as it always does, Charlie is bored. I know very little about oriental cats, having been used to moggies all my life, but I am learning fast. Charlie has typical Siamese features, slanting blue olives for eyes, a tapering muzzle, large rotating ears and a long prehensile-looking tail. Dense hard muscles rippled under his short-haired coat, which is a rich brown overall – Havana brown, according to George. It is a name that smacks of Cuban cigars or coffee. Charlie is svelte, elegant and proud, and he can hunt.

'A great rabbiter,' George says evenly, rolling his Rs in the way southern New Zealanders are apt to. He speaks with an assurance that comes from living on ancestral acres for 60-something years and knowing intimately how things work around here.

'How great?' I ask.

'Well, he's five years old now. I'd say he's killed, let's see, five hundred rabbits or so all told. Mostly young ones. He catches them when they emerge from their burrows out on the dunes. Hunts day or night.'

Like his high-brow name, Charlie is a star act. I look into those knowing eyes again. The pupils are vertical slits that no doubt enlarge in the dark to become round, black and deadly. In old Siam these cats were bred to guard temples, says George. Charlie pads silently into the kitchen next door and we hear him scuffling with his brother, who is black overall and nothing like the pampered-looking white Siamese, the ones with dark points. Next there is the sound of pawing at old newspaper lying crumpled beside the log burner.

'He wants me to light the fire,' says George. 'He'll have to wait. I'm repairing the chimney today'

Among oriental cats at least, feline intelligence and perception can take the breath away. The wooden doorknobs in the McIntosh home are deeply scratched from claw marks made by

Charlie and his brothers. They can open the doors. They do this by standing on their long back legs, grasping the doorknob with their front claws and twisting. Clever as you like. I try a doorknob. It turns only with a deliberate twist of the wrist.

The sea lions can wait a few moments more while I pursue the question of Siamese IQ. It so happens George has researched the topic. I might have known.

'It's got a lot to do with the way their brains have developed. Cats' brains are very convoluted.'

'Convoluted?'

'You know, the way our own brains are built, with folds and winding ridges. It's similar in cats, but on a smaller scale. I've read that the convolutions have got something to do with increasing the surface area. The greater the surface area the higher the intelligence.'

Now we are at the nitty-gritty of it. Siamese are adept at hunting and door-opening, and practically capable of a running conversation with humans, because of this special brain development. I make a mental note somewhere among the convolutions of my own grey matter to research brains further some time. Charlie is back, scratching the upholstery of my chair and muttering something.

'Do you think he'll mind if we talk about sea lions for a while?' I ask.

George answers something to the effect the sea lions do not much interest Charlie, they are not his type. So sea lions it is.

We delight in discussing sea lions, George and I. Taieri Mouth is not a regular haul-out site for them but it now has a place forever in the annals of sea lion activity on the New Zealand mainland because of the birth of a pup at the end of 1993 – the first recorded birth since the disappearance of sea lions from the mainland 400 years ago. The mother chose the shrubland and marram-covered dunes in front of George and Juliet McIntosh's place for the historic event. She chose well. George kept a friendly eye on her – and an eye out for threats such as stray dogs and tearaways on trailbikes.

The birth occurred around Christmas time. No one witnessed the event but George had seen the sea lion on the beach for a few weeks beforehand. She used to lounge on the beach between bouts of foraging at sea. It was George who first reported the pup. Two years later the same female returned and gave birth to a second pup about a kilometre up the river and on the north bank again. It is a wildlife phenomenon. Sea lions coming home. Two births hardly makes a colony, but it is a start. The mother taught her pups to swim at a young age then coaxed them north past Brighton and the long sweep of sand to Otago Peninsula, the wild side of Dunedin. It must have been an exhausting journey for pups so young.

From time to time I keep in touch with George about whether any more sea lions have hauled out at Taieri Mouth. Few seem to bother. Otago Peninsula, on the other hand, jutting into the Pacific Ocean north of Taieri Mouth, is a favoured hauling ground. You might find 10 to 20 sea lions at a time on some of the beaches there, mostly males. Today, for want of something different to do, I half hoped conditions would allow me to walk to an island that lies on the seaward side of the river mouth. Islands are like mountaintops to me. They are aloof and alluring. They speak of remoteness and independence, of nature doing its own thing. They certainly have personality. No two islands are the same.

Maps call this one Taieri Island, after the river. It has another name, Moturata – Rata Island. Sometimes a sandbank is exposed at low tide, connecting the island to the mainland. Right now, though, the sea has severed the connection so that even at low tide the gap between island and mainland is awash, a tangle of waves churning and cutting across one another. The island, 500 metres long and up to 250 metres wide, lies about a kilometre off the mouth of the Taieri River and immediately opposite it. You would swear Baxter's 'old water-dragon', sliding out of its 'stone gullet' gorge, had long ago developed a lump in its throat and spat it out, creating Moturata. The island was hurled an awkward distance, too far for a sand bar to form permanently. As a result, the river is at times a two-headed dragon at its mouth, with the flow split by the island. The sea, however, the 'always talking sea' of Baxter's poetry, never leaves things alone for long, and sooner or later, on one side or the other, a sandbank will build up and join the island to the mainland at low tide.

George McIntosh walked to the island several times as a youngster when the sandbank was exposed on the north side of the mouth, the McIntosh side. On one occasion, not yet a teenager, he went alone. He became absorbed by things on the island and had to scamper back with the tide coming in and water lapping high on his legs. His father, Hugh, saw him take the risk. When George emerged from the water, his dad was on the beach waiting for him, with a whippy stick in his hand. He gave George a thrashing.

The commercial fishermen whose boats are based at the Taieri Mouth jetties, a respectful distance back from the mouth, refer to the north bar and south bar when discussing safe passage through the mouth and past the island. They can get a thrashing, too. They know from the wrecks and drownings of the past that the bars are death to the unwary. Of all the fishing ports on the Otago coast, this one has the trickiest entrance. Although today's fishing boats are faster and more powerful than the old-timers, you need to know more than just what the tide is doing. You need to be able to read the lift and lurch of the swells, the whack and wallop of the wind and the surreptitious sweep of rips and currents.

Leaving or entering Taieri Mouth, you need to have your personal radar tuned to the elements, and go for it when the moment seizes you. The sea is not in the business of pleasing or accommodating. It just is.

Many boats have come to grief here. The earliest record is that of the schooner *Dublin Packet*, which was hurled on to a reef in 1839 by the sudden arrival of a mighty set of rollers. She had been trying to land stores for the whaling station then located on the island. Three men lost their lives. When Taieri Mouth became a conduit for miners and settlers in the Central Otago gold rush of the 1860s, the toll mounted. Pilots were posted to the island in the interests of safety. Napi Point, the northern lip of Taieri Mouth, a landmark on the McIntosh property, is named after a 12-metre schooner that was driven ashore in a south-west gale in 1860 laden with goods for a group of Milton settlers. Taieri Mouth people are long used to combing the beaches for things washed up.

George McIntosh is steadily whittling salvaged kauri timbers into utensils and keepsakes. The kauri is from the vessel *Pansy*, which was wrecked on the north bar in the autumn of 1940 while coming back from a fishing trip. The Tunnage brothers, Tom and Bob, were drowned. Bob's body floated to the island and was found there four days later. Local people could hardly believe it: no drowning victims had ever washed up on the island in their experience. It was the last place you looked. But the Tunnage boys' mother had a dream one night that Bob was on the island. She implored local fishermen to go and have a look. They did so without any sort of hope. Bob was there all right, still wearing his gumboots and heavy fisherman's apron. Three weeks after the capsize the other brother's body came to light on a beach at Kuri Bush, just up the road from the McIntoshes.

Kuri Bush has a poetic ring to it, if only because this was where Jim Baxter spent his preschool years. His poem, 'At Kuri Bush', offers a rare glimpse of a nostalgic Baxter. Usually he is strident, sardonic, incisive and insightful. On a visit to the site of his old home, since demolished, he souvenirs a chip of the chimney. It becomes a sort of security symbol. Before they moved to Brighton, the Baxters had the farm next door to the McIntoshes. George's father, Hugh, always said the Baxters were great neighbours. These were the 'pitching' days, when neighbours would visit to pitch a yarn: the days before a decent road and electric light. The countryside was a swaying sea of oats and potato tops, with weka cooeeing like shrill-voiced Aussies from pockets of bush, and cattle going down to the beach to wrap supple lips around the stranded kelp. After World War I, Hugh McIntosh had gone blacksmithing, shearing and rabbiting to set himself up before taking over the family farm. They were neighbourly days all right. Mrs Baxter arrived at the McIntosh house one day with baby James in a pram. As she approached the verandah, Hugh stepped forward to lift the pram up the steps. Mrs Baxter told him not to bother, but before she could explain the collapsible design of the pram, Hugh wrapped his hefty arms around the pram, baby and all. Suddenly, the pram began collapsing in on the baby, and Hugh had to quickly put it down or risk injuring the future bard.

In George's time, there were cows to milk and horses to harness but eventually the farm became the domain of sheep, and George carried on sheep farming when it was his turn to manage the hills flanking river and sea.

The settler McIntoshes arrived in Otago from Scotland on New Year's Day in the year of the Gabriel's Gully goldrush, 1861. George's grandfather, also George, was a nine-year-old at the time, the son of Hugh. McIntoshes have alternated Hugh, George, Hugh, George for generations. In the early 1880s, grandfather George put a stake in the ground at Taieri Mouth by buying 100 acres from the southern chief Hori Kerei Taiaroa for six pounds ten shillings an acre. The farm, added to later, was cut out of a Maori reserve that dated from the 1844 Otago settlement deal. Reserve land extended along the north bank of the river as far as Henley, about eight kilometres inland. The settlers called it Maori ground. So did Baxter, and the vernacular lives on. George McIntosh still uses the term. He is Taieri Mouth to the core.

George's family tree goes back to the first European settlers here. Grandfather George married Susan Morgan, who was said to be the first white woman born at Taieri Mouth. Her mother, Agnes Macdonald, arrived in 1851 with her parents and two sisters. When the Macdonalds reached Taieri Mouth, a thickset ferryman greeted them. As he lifted the oldest daughter, Mary Ellen, out of the boat that day, he told her she was the first white woman to set foot on Taieri Beach.

TWO

LEGENDARY CHARACTERS seem to spring more easily from the sea than from the land. Why is this? What is it about the sea that cultivates character? Sea-dogs and old salts. Is it the estranging, unpredictable nature of deep ocean, a frothing rage one day, voluptuously smooth the next? If you can cope with these sorts of swings in the elements, you can cope with anything. Lyricists have had a fine old time exploring the sea's nature and its impact on human values. W.B. Yeats wrote of the sea's 'murderous innocence', Longfellow revelled in the 'sea-tides tossing free', and Coleridge's Ancient Mariner is forever riding the waves of sea lore. So much for the surface, but what about deeper down? Serpents and monsters recur in the mythology of the sea. If the Taieri River is an old water-dragon sliding to the sea, as Baxter suggests, what manner of serpents inhabit the ocean deep, couched there waiting to test the mettle of mariners?

A character who emerged from the whaling era of the early 19th century now haunts the history of Taieri Mouth. John Bull arrived just in time to carry George McIntosh's great-great-aunt ashore. But he carried more than people during his ferryman days. He carried a mysterious past. Once a whaler, he probably always saw himself as a man of the sea even though he turned to the Taieri River for a living. Toss in his no-frills lifestyle ashore, his impressive physique and awesome strength, and you have the stuff of which legends are made. He was straight out of a storybook.

'John Bull will get you.'

'John Bull will cut you up for fish bait.'

Taieri Mouth children were fed comments like this in the mid-1800s. The old whaler was the ogre in a home-grown fairytale, a terrifying prospect for any youngster. With few children's books at the disposal of the settlers, a parent could be excused for embellishing the yarns about John Bull. Most children, though, grew to realise he had a kindly nature beneath the austere countenance and the red whiskers a foot and a half long. Bare feet were a trademark of his. When he did wear boots he left them unlaced – the better to bail boats with. He would have been about 40 years of age when he came to the Mouth to set himself up as the ferryman. He was already an enigmatic figure. For a start, he had several names. John Bull was a nickname and few people knew any other. But when officialdom came calling, he was inclined to give the surname Williams . . . or O'Neill. When he married a Maori woman from the community upstream at Henley, he is reported to have said for registry purposes, 'You had better put down Williams.'

As for his nickname, it seems he acquired it on a whaling ship. About the age of seven, so the story goes, he was kidnapped by whaling interests on the east coast of North America and given the name of the stereotypical Englishman, notwithstanding his claim to Irish ancestry (someone would later argue the laceless boots confirmed his Irishness). In the 1830s, he turned up at the Weller Brothers' shore whaling station at Otakou in Otago Harbour. Soon his whaling days would be behind him because the whales were disappearing fast. A career move was indicated. John Bull next earned a living by fishing and boating on the harbour. His abode was a cave near the Otago Heads where he lived, according to a contemporary, 'in a manner foreign to civilised custom'. But after the first immigrant ships arrived in 1848, he decided the harbour was becoming too crowded and he must move on. South he went to Henley to work as a boatman on the Taieri River. When cattle needed to be driven across the river, John Bull dispensed with the boat and swam with them. He was a strong swimmer, strong at everything. He could swim across the river with his clothes balanced on his head. As for a roof over his head, he had simple tastes. An upturned whaleboat did the trick for a while.

At Henley he married a local woman, Apaikai. To his great dismay she died after a few years, and from there the John Bull story moves to the Mouth. Downstream of the Henley ferry, the river is broad and slow, offering an easy ride by boat to the Mouth. For an old whaler, the Mouth just had to be the next best thing to a life at sea. The Mouth was thoroughly tidal, and over at Taieri Island you could smell where the whales had been hauled and flensed.

Like the John Bull cartoon figure, our man was stocky, but there the similarity ended. The ferryman was roughly dressed and gruffly spoken. He smoked a short clay pipe that reeked of tarry tobacco. Of powerful build, he astonished local people with his feats of strength and daring. Imagine a breezy day on the coast north of Taieri Mouth. John Bull is boating to the Mouth from Dunedin and puts in at Brighton because the sea is becoming a bit too challenging for his little boat. She is taking on water. Instead of waiting for calmer weather, he decides to proceed on foot. There is no road; the sea is the highway. A picture of obstinate self-sufficiency, he simply picks up the boat and starts marching down the beaches with it – a story told by the lady who gave him a cup of tea about the halfway mark. At the river mouth he launches the boat and is soon home. They say he carried a 200-pound bag of flour all the way from Dunedin to Balclutha in the early days, and that if he did not have a load on his back it was because he was travelling in ballast, so to speak, and on his way to his next Herculean assignment.

John Bull survived numerous logging and boating mishaps. He fell from a tree one time without hurting much more than his pride. When Governor Grey paid an official visit to Taieri Mouth in 1867, the ferryman decided to fire a vice-regal salute from a cannon; unfortunately, it blew up in his face. By one account, it had been booby-trapped with stones. He suffered deep gashes to his leg and face but little else. He seemed indestructible. In his latter years he broke his arm and spent time in hospital. Something else cracked about that time, something intangible. Perhaps he saw the changes that were coming to Taieri Mouth with a motor road, more intensive farming, flax-milling and so on, and the thought of it all depressed him. A worried community rallied round, held fundraising concerts and built a new hut to replace his leaking, draughty shack. It is said he suffered cancer of the mouth in his latter years, a result of the pipe perhaps. He died on Christmas Eve 1883 at the age (estimated) of 73. John Bull was buried upriver in the Henley cemetery alongside his wife. His grave, like many others there, is unmarked.

Characters like John Bull are sometimes turned into legends after they've gone; John Bull, though, was a legend in his own lifetime. You can sense his impact from the procession of landmarks named for him at Taieri Mouth or in the gorge: John Bull's Camp, John Bull's Head, John Bull's Gully, and John Bull's Upper Garden. Some of these names have been overlaid on existing Maori ones. You walk with a legend when you take the track up the gorge.

THREE

LIKE MANY OTHER Maori names in the landscape, Taieri represents the first poetry of the land. Taieri is a variant of Taiari, a word that, by one translation at least, refers to a certain tide. Maori survived by their knowledge of natural processes and had names for each tide, from new moon through to full moon. Taiari was the eleventh tide of the moon. From such a name you might assume the river is strongly influenced by the tide. And it is. At spring tides when the river is low, the salt can penetrate ten kilometres inland, although it is well diluted by then. Flounders are common upstream of the gorge. On rare occasions fur seals have swum as far as Allanton, 20 kilometres upriver. Either the seals are partial to the taste of trout or they are especially adventurous and do not know when to turn back.

Whereas a seal can go upriver for a day and come back to rest on Moturata's rocky shoreline till it feels hungry again, I am a terrestrial being. On this mid-winter's day with the sea wreathing the island on every side with surf or choppy water, making it inaccessible, I must settle for a stroll into the gorge and John Bull country. The walkway sets out from the south bank upstream of the river bridge. No need for punts these days. Completed in 1980, the bridge is almost 200 metres long. Two lanes of tarseal, mounted on massive concrete piles and beams, link the north bank with the south. It is an open invitation to city folk to pour into the place. John Bull would have had a fit. Driving across the bridge, you need to keep your wits about you. Visually, there is a lot of water to lap up – the river emerging from its gorge, the churning mouth, and the sea beyond. From this angle, the island appears as a flattened cone, an eroded Rangitoto. But unlike the young volcanic Rangitoto, which guards Auckland's Waitemata Harbour, Taieri Island is built of ancient metamorphic rock. It marks the edge of a split in the earth's crust, the Akatore Fault, which passes to the seaward side of the island and is capable of rattling the windows on Taieri Mouth cribs and houses from time to time.

Actually, it feels like earthquake weather right now. The still air hangs heavily. The sky is draped with clouds that are going nowhere, all tucks and billows like an old-style theatre curtain waiting to unveil a dramatic performance. Pastel hues between red and orange tint the bulging parts as the solstice sun tries to break through and light up the stage. The sun's low angle at this time of year can produce a sunset sky in the middle of the day.

The only things moving apart from the ebbing water are the fishing boats, which gently nudge the wooden jetties, and the red-billed gulls rotating in the air above the boats, ever watchful for sign of fish guts cast into the water. Enscribing black-and-white question marks with their looping necks, the little shags are statue-still on the wooden piles that used to support the old bridge. With the patience of cormorants, they wait for a feed to swim by. Some of them have their wings stretched to dry. When you see them like this, imitating pterodactyls, you are reminded of the long ancestry of birds.

At the south end of the bridge I turn away from the sea and drive along a side road past a line of riverside cribs, all neat and shipshape, to reach the start of the walkway. The river is broad and mud-brown at this point. I set out along the track, bundled up against the bite in the air. Where this river begins you would need thermal gear – and skis – at this time of year. The river rises in the Lammermoor and Lammerlaw Ranges of Central Otago as seepages, string bogs and small streams ribboning vast areas of snow tussock a thousand metres above sea level. It is easy on the eye, this landscape, filled with soft curves. There are no trees, no sharp edges. Except for the wet patches, everything is a uniform tawny or golden colour, depending on the light, and furry to behold. The tussock clumps are chest-high to walk through.

Tumbling quickly to the Maniototo's flat land, the river performs the most extraordinary dance – a whirling, coiling performance that leaves the upper part of the plain ornately inscribed with channels, levees and backwaters. You would travel a long way to see anything like it. Further downstream, with the riverdance behind it, the Taieri behaves more predictably. It does a U-turn around the end of the Rock and Pillar Range, shoots through the Hyde Gorge, runs steadily down the Strath Taieri Valley then plunges into its middle gorge to reach the lower Taieri. Now its pace is slower. The river is generally broader, and browner. And 300 kilometres wiser. In New Zealand, only the Waikato and Clutha Rivers journey farther. Salt is starting to infiltrate. Like all rivers, the Taieri cannot resist the salt. Salt is its addiction and its destiny.

George McIntosh tells me that the Taieri used to run with less sediment, and that gold mining – historical as well as present-day ventures – together with erosion arising from more intensive land use upcountry, are responsible for an increase in the murkiness of the water. As a result, he says, mudflats have replaced the beaches of creamy sand that once formed the river's edges in the vicinity of the bridge. There have been changes in the vegetation, too.

Marram grass and lupins were introduced in the 1920s to stabilise the sand dunes, displacing the picturesque pingao, a native sand-binding sedge whose leaves are a glorious golden-orange and whose dark-brown flowerheads spiral in an artistic manner. The lupins did well at the beginning but have succumbed to a fungal disease in recent years, leaving the marram to proliferate on the dunelands. Gorse, which came before the marram, is another invasive plant, literally a thorn in the side of many farmers. Actually, it was introduced as a sand binder along the United States east coast, where it is called furze. It was brought here for hedgerows. In the absence of things that eat it and keep it in check back home in Britain and western Europe, it has invaded large tracts of disturbed land and pastoral country. In southern New Zealand it has gone berserk, flowering madly even in the middle of winter. All you can say in its favour is that it is a nitrogen fixer and doing the soil some good, and if native trees can establish within the leguminous gorse, they will overtop and eventually shade it out. For gorse loves the sun. As its pods crack open in the heat, the small black seeds are fired out. They are real survivors. Gorse seed can sit in the ground for decades, waiting for a chance to germinate.

    Turning a corner on the track, I encounter a belt of gorse flanking both sides of the track. It is in full flower, garishly at odds with the season and filling the air with its cloying scent. I press on towards a patch of native bush. It is humid under the canopy and frost-free. Temperatures are moderated in an evergreen forest. There's really only one season here – autumn. The forest floor is a palette of autumn colours, browns, reds, and yellows, the glorious colours of decay. But leaf fall is more than a pretty picture; it is also instructive. To identify what is forming the canopy above you, look down, look at the leaf litter under your feet.

    On the track ahead, though, is something that looks anything but autumnal. It is from a plant that is as symbolic of indigenous flora as gorse is symbolic of invasive problem plants. Upturned on the track, as if plucked from an All Black rugby jersey, is the tip of a silver fern frond. It is not every day you encounter the silver fern in the raw, and no doubt a lot of people stroll past the plant without recognising it, for its upper surface is green just like other tree ferns. In this forest, the main players are mahoe, kamahi, broadleaf, tree fuchsia and an occasional totara left over from logging days. There are ferns galore – soft tree fern, the necklace-like Blechnums and the endearing hen-and-chickens fern, so named because of the tiny light-green miniature ferns that sprout from the mature fronds and drop off to make new plants. But I was not expecting to see silver fern.

The bird calls here are also surprising; more precisely, it is the mix of bird calls that astonishes. On entering a forest like this you naturally listen out for the calls of bush birds like bellbird, tui, fantail, grey warbler and brown creeper, most of which you will hear before you see. Hearing the prolonged trilling of the brown creepers is a special treat, one worth pausing for. They strike five or six notes in their full song. In a few moments, you might catch sight of an extended family of them trickling through the canopy like airborne mice and just as hungry for insects as mice. Toss in the melodic call of a bellbird and the sweet chatter of a fantail, and you begin to feel at home in the forest. But what is that discordant screeching over by the river? It jars on the ear; it does not fit here. It is more a coastal sound. Some black-backed gulls are tracking up the gorge on an inland mission.

The gulls are not the only birds to use the gorge as a thoroughfare. Through a gap in the trees I see a black shag, largest of the New Zealand cormorants, heading upriver, wings a blur. You wonder what motivates them. All our shags fly with the speed and purpose of carrier pigeons. What is the hurry? Are they late for an appointment somewhere? Has the avian wireless called all cormorants to a humdinger of a fishing spot? Black shags have a taste for river fish. Propelled underwater by their big webbed feet, they can stay submerged for up to a minute. Mullet, flounder and sea-run trout are among the fish they target in these last few kilometres of the river, but you can expect to see them anywhere along it, from the scroll plain to the craggy gorges and the plains. Anglers curse them.

Not all the traffic is aerial and heading up the river. The black shag has passed the rounded islet known as John Bull's Head, which is close to the opposite bank, and begun turning into the start of an S-bend on the river, when I notice something moving on the water.

Through the trees I make out a small boat heading downriver. It is a canoe or maybe a kayak. Whoever is paddling the craft has it moving swiftly, even allowing for the ebbing tide. Canoe and paddler make a smooth, compact unit, skimming along with the tide. I wonder how far they have come and whether I will see them heading back soon?

A boat ride through the gorge at weekends or in the summer holidays was just the thing in the late 1800s. Little steam-driven launches based at Henley would connect with steam trains from Dunedin for a full day's outing. Henley was a proper little tourist village, well pleased to develop a boating tradition along the lines of its River Thames namesake in England. On a busy day up to 400 pleasure-seekers bound for Taieri Mouth would crowd the decks of the launches. It was standing room only on some trips. There would be a law against such crowding today. Without exception, the travellers had on their Sunday best, the women in bonnets and long dresses, the men in bow ties. Puffing locomotives shuttled them back and forth from the city. As the local newspaper reported in December 1880: 'The river is gay with boats in which numerous picnic parties have come to spend the day.' At the Mouth, they had a choice of recreational pursuits. They could walk in the 'cool inviting bush' as I am doing, bathe well covered in the surf, or simply promenade on the slick hard sand of Taieri Beach. During the working week, the launches transported freight. Fertiliser, cement, coal and other supplies headed down through the gorge to the village and farms. Oats, chaff, potatoes and timber came back up. No such trade occurs today. Henley is a backwater, although a tourist launch service based at Taieri Mouth has been trying to restore the pleasure-cruise tradition.

There would have been no pleasure, however, for anyone cruising the gorge on a certain night in 1960. A tsunami hit the Otago coast, the product of an undersea earthquake on the other side of the Pacific, somewhere off Chile. It struck in the early morning, waking George McIntosh, who was then living in the old family home at the edge of a low cliff overlooking the mouth. He remembers the sound of water crashing and rumbling, remembers thinking the noise very odd. The night was not stormy and the tide should have been out at that time. Up at the wharves, boats broke loose in the darkness. A launch built for gorge trips was picked up by the huge surge and badly damaged when it collided with the bridge. At daybreak, the locals looked disbelievingly at the imprint of the tsunami, which in those days was mistakenly called a tidal wave. This was no whim of the tide. Half a kilometre above the bridge, that is, about two kilometres from the mouth, you could see debris hung up in the trees. The wave could have been five metres high as it swept into the gorge. Flounders, cast well up into the rushes, were left stranded when the water level dropped suddenly.

Looking down on the river from the walking track, I try to imagine such an event – the advancing wall of water, the damage to boats and wharves. There were aftershocks just like in an earthquake. Water levels in the river rose and fell out of step with the tides. At intervals the sea would flow over the jetties and swamp beaches unused to such high tides, and just as suddenly it would drain away as if disappearing down some oceanic plughole. Only on the fourth day did the tides return to normal. Out at sea, a tsunami is often disguised by the swells. It may be a wave only half a metre high. But it is likely to be travelling at breathtaking speed. As much as 800 kilometres an hour – as fast as a modern jet aircraft. All you might notice in a deep-sea fishing boat is an extra lurch, nothing startling. But as the wave reaches a continental shelf and shallow coastal waters, it slows. The energy has to go somewhere. The wave rears up.

In 1868 another seismic sea wave swept through the gorge. This was a big one, and it occurred in daylight hours. Antonio Joseph, a whaler and skipper of coastal vessels who kept an accommodation house at Henley at one time, was in a small vessel upstream of the gorge when the wave came through. It took hold of his boat and lifted it over the riverbank. When the water receded he and the boat were left high and dry. He walked back to the Maori village at Henley to find the people there in a state of panic. When their huts had been flooded, they took to a nearby hill, an old pa site, and refused to come down for some time in case the sea charged back again. Earthquakes and tsunamis, like the eclipses of the sun, are mortifying phenomena. They are wake-up calls for anyone who thinks humans are wholly in control of nature.

I burst out of the dim forest and into a patch of midwinter sunlight. Having gained height I have a view back towards the coast and the river's final writhing before it meets the sea. There is a cloud shadow across the river. The canoe is in the frame but no more significant now than a piece of driftwood.

Farther on, at the high point of the track some 200 metres above the river, there is a seat. From here you can see a large tract of coastline, as far north as the soaring dunes of Sandfly Bay, where the sand really does fly in a southerly. North of Brighton and a few kilometres offshore, Green Island is a black shark fin angling through a silver sea. The view inland is all hills and mountains, wave after wave. Faintly in the distance is the summit crest of the Rock and Pillar Range, the edge of Central Otago. Something is missing for this time of year – the glint of snow. Reflecting a mild winter, the range is a hazy dark-blue. Immediately below and out of sight is John Bull's Gully, which, after a drink and a breather, I make for, slithering my way down the steep track.

The fabled gully turns out to be narrow, steep-sided and V-shaped. It has a tucked-away feel to it. Did John Bull's potatoes get flooded in the great wave of 1868? There is no record of what he was doing at the time, but if it required brute strength he would probably be in the thick of it. The jetty that once welcomed scores of picnickers with their mutton sandwiches and rhubarb pies has gone. A hundred years ago the launches pulled in here with people who had no idea whatever of nuclear weapons, jet aircraft, television, traffic lights, agrichemicals, Aids or the Internet. It was a serene era, and seemingly innocent. On a day as calm and crisply tuned as this one, you can sample the serenity. The river slides by in silence, saving its secrets. On the north-facing wall of the gully, kowhai trees are starting to produce their spring flowers a month or two early, exciting the gully's bellbirds and tui to seek a nectar snack. The birds are noisy and bossy. A New Zealand pigeon joins them, wings whistling. A fruit pigeon with tropical origins but with few fruits to chose from in the southern New Zealand forest in winter, it will gobble the dangling canary-yellow kowhai flowers whole.

Is that the picnickers' laughter I hear? Or merely the chuckling of a troupe of brown creepers as they perform their acrobatic routines in the canopy? Congenial birds, brown creepers. You often see them flocking with silvereyes, grey warblers and fantails. For them, every day is a picnic. Judging by the thickly matted grass, John Bull's Gully is not as popular as it once was, although it retains an old-world charm. Narrow-leaved lacebarks and lowland ribbonwoods are the shade trees. On steep slopes above the gully, out of reach of loggers, mature specimens of rimu, matai and totara stand out above the forest canopy. The skyline is where old New Zealand meets progress. Looming into view is the edge of a plantation of pines. These are Monterey pines, *Pinus radiata*, native to California's Monterey Peninsula. They have certainly radiated in this country. Monterey has also given us a cypress, used originally as shelterbelts in New Zealand. We commonly refer to it by its species name, macrocarpa.

In the 1950s George McIntosh planted a row of macrocarpas on the foreshore near his family home. He wanted to create some shelter and something different to look at on the shoreline apart from the invasive lupins. The trees are two-look trees today. You need two looks to reach the top of them with your eye. Closely planted, they are about as tall as macrocarpas grow anywhere, yet they are standing on sand. You do not often see this. As I plunge into the forest for the walk back to the sea air, I make a note to ask George about his seaside cypresses.

FOUR

THE ANSWER LIES in the soil or, in this case, in the sand. Macrocarpa trees planted in sand develop a massively deep and intricate root system in contrast to the shallow root plates of macrocarpa planted in heavy soils.

'You won't see these trees blow over in a hurry,' says George.

I take his word for it. The trees are family. George grew some of them from seed that he collected locally. Trees, birds, fish, seals

– George has grown up with them all around here. The afternoon is wearing on, still calm and mostly grey. The view from George's place over the dunes, river mouth, surf zone and island tempts me to check the beach for sea lions before I head home to Otago Peninsula, about an hour's drive from here. Sea lions can turn up at any time. You never know when they will emerge from the sea and lumber purposefully across the sand, creating a scalloped trail of flipperprints as they go.

On this Taieri Mouth beach, you need to look carefully. Pieces of driftwood lie like sleeping animals. The beach is the final resting place of trees wrenched by flood or landslip from banks somewhere upriver. Most of the logs are rubbed smooth and weathered to a silver-grey colour not unlike the colour of an adult female sea lion. Nothing is moving today, though, except for the oystercatchers. Jet-black beachcombers with orange-red bills, they walk briskly about their business, turning over stranded seaweed and shells and leaving probe holes in the sand. The tide is almost fully out; their table is laid.

Leaving the logs to the firewood gatherers and those who look at driftwood for more than sea lion shapes, I cut back along the sandy shores of the river, past George's macrocarpas, cathedral tall. I am trying to remember what he said about a couple of rata trees that once grew on the edge of the river near here. Apparently the river is a natural boundary for rata, which is common to the south but suddenly becomes scarce on the north side. In the case of ngaio, a coastal tree that forms billowing canopies, the opposite is true. Ngaio are common beside the Brighton road to the north of Taieri Mouth but they disappear south of the river.

Now my attention is distracted from biogeography to boats. Up ahead, hauled out on the sand a few metres above the ebbing tide, is a boat, possibly the canoe I saw in the gorge earlier in the day. It is a deep purple colour, over three metres long. Graceful curves in the design smack of modern technology. There is no sign of a paddle – or the paddler. I move in for a closer look.

'Ahoy!'

The voice is firm but not unfriendly. For a moment it seems to be coming from inside the canoe.

'You out there without a paddle!'

I know the voice but not well enough to place its owner immediately.

'... *without a paddle*'. Phrase and intonation nag at me till an image crystallises. The Lark. Could it be the Lark? What is this high-country character doing here? He hailed me like this one summer's day a few years ago at Sutton Salt Lake in the Strath Taieri. At the time I was exploring the lake, then as parched and cracked as a Saharan water hole. The Lark – a name derived from Alec, mispronounced when he was a child – had been resting in the shade of a schist tor beside the salt pan. He yelled a sailor's greeting then, and here he is doing the same thing – from a cave of a different sort. This time his cave is a sandy-floored hollow at the base of the cliffs a metre or so above normal high tides. I can see it is half-filled with tangled driftwood, heaped there presumably when high spring tides coincide with a storm surge or a flood.

The Lark has talked of 'wearing the land' in the past. Here his dark-green bush jacket merges with the ferns and mosses on the cave wall. Overhanging native tree daisies and shore hebes are battling with golden gorse on the cliff above.

'How's tricks?' he says as I walk up to meet him.

'I'm stunned and amazed.' I knew him as an itinerant farm hand with Border collie at heel, blade shears in the back pocket and a hang glider stashed in the hills so he could go joy-riding with a falcon he rescued as a chick.

From his seated position, legs crossed meditatively under the

Swanndri, the Lark proffers a powerful weathered hand. It is a no-nonsense shearer's handshake. I remember the pale-blue eyes, the colour of high-country sky in a nor'wester, and the ginger complexion. A ginger stubble covers his chin. Because he is not wearing his trademark denim cap I notice his light ginger hair has grown paler. He must be well into his fifties by now.

'Well, you're a bolt out of the blue,' I say. 'What brings you here?'

'A Pirouette.'

I frown at him.

'My kayak. Pirouette is the name of the model. Good for running the river and sampling the surf. Keeps me fit.'

'Last time I saw you, you were into hang gliders. Hooked on them, as I remember. What's a high-country man doing at the coast?'

'Nothing's changed. I'm still a glider pilot, only of late I've taken to the water as well. Wind and water – great elements to explore by.'

With that, the Lark begins to explain his trips to the coast. When the mood takes him and weather conditions suit, he flies his glider to a predetermined point in the river's middle gorge, handy to where he has cached his kayak. Often it will be around the Hindon area. From there, it is all downhill, so to speak, if a little wet and frisky in places. Getting back can be challenging and at times he has to portage the kayak and gear when the rapids are too tough. He says winter trips are rare. He can reach the coast, by air and water, in a day, although he camps out in the bush along the way on some trips.

'Saw you in the gorge earlier,' I say.

The Lark reaches for a handful of sand and lets it trickle free.

'I'm following a natural cycle seaward,' he says.

Meeting a puzzled look from me, he goes on. 'This sand here

is from Central Otago. Quartz sand from the schist country, washed down the Clutha River and carried up the coast by tidal currents. It's taking a break at the seaside. Just like me. Fancy a tea?'

I notice then he has a little gas cooker sheltering behind him, noiselessly heating a blackened billy.

'It'll have to be black,' he says, reaching over to check the billy. 'Couldn't get the hang of your fruit teas.'

He is referring to the first time we met, on a lonely road on the outskirts of Middlemarch. He came by on foot whistling a Scottish tune while I was sitting in my ageing Commer camper van near an intriguing hill called Smooth Cone. I invited him to step aboard and offered him a rosehip tea.

The Lark has not moved from his cross-legged position. I join him on the sand. It is cool but dry.

'My idea of a camper van, a cave like this,' he says. 'Bit of history to it, like your old van.'

The way the Lark tells it, the cave was used by the man who surveyed the original Otago settlement and bought the whole block from Maori chiefs for 2,400 pounds sterling: one Frederick Tuckett. I had come across Tuckett's name in my meandering through Taieri Mouth history, but I did not realise he camped in this cave in the course of his 1844 reconnaissance. He and his companion, Dr David Monro, walked from Henley with sleet showers falling – an irrational thing to do when a boat could have transported him to the Mouth in a fraction of the time. One source described him quaintly as 'an excellent pedestrian'. The record also suggests his Taieri Mouth visit was an ordeal. 'Grumbling all night on the beach,' he wrote in his diary, a reference to the lengths he went to – with fires and gunfire – to signal his presence to the whalers living on the island.

'A funny coot, Tuckett,' says the Lark. 'Short-tempered.'

'Why do you think he walked from Henley when he could have borrowed a boat?'

'History books say no boat was available. But I've an idea he didn't hit if off with the local Maori and they refused to lend one.' For a moment the Lark gazes out at the old Taieri sliding past. 'Go with the flow, that's my motto. Tuckett seemed to be pushing the river.'

It is an appropriate time to ask the Lark about his own craft, given that I know little about kayaks.

'Simple,' says the Lark. 'A kayak has a waterproof cockpit; a canoe is much more open. You can go places in a kayak you could never take a canoe. On some of the Taieri River rapids you'd be swamped straight off. Kayak is a North American invention, an Inuit word, in fact. I thought a wordsmith would know that.'

'Makes sense,' I say, non-committally.

'Actually, kayaks paddled by women had another name: umiak. The Inuit built frames of whalebone or wood and stretched animal skins across them. They often used seal skins. Used the skins for all sorts of things – clothing, boots, bags, dog traces, the bone for knives, the oil for heat and lighting.'

'What about your own boat? What's it made of?'

'She's plastic. Moulded plastic, polyethelene, I think. Not too dusty, eh? The seating's solid foam. The paddle here,' – he points out a racy looking paddle leaning against the driftwood, with bright yellow blades, a far cry from my Brighton canoeing days – 'it's made of aluminium, fibreglass inlays and carbon. All very high-tech'. He pauses, reflective. 'It's not the hull that keeps you afloat. It's the space within. That's the useful bit.'

The Lark hands me a steaming mug. The tea is darker than I'd normally take it, but I go with the flow.

'That'll warm the bivalves,' he says.

'Bivalves?'

'Cockles.'

The Lark is the sort of self-contained person who seems wasted on himself, a light-hearted loner who would no more grumble all night than abandon his Swanni. He travels light, for sure. The kayak has just enough storage space behind the seat for a tent or fly, sleeping bag, little gas cooker, billy and a few provisions. I ask him if he ever ventures out to sea.

'Too right. But you know, the river's one thing, the sea's another. I'm still learning its quirks and secrets. There's a lot of power and emotion out there. Ocean emotion. It pays to be wary. On a really fine day I might hot-paddle it to Brighton. Mostly, though, I potter about the island and ride the breakers to keep my hand in. One thing, though, you won't find me hanging about here when there's lots of people around.'

'You sound like John Bull, an old character from round here. Heard of him? He spent a lifetime keeping out of the road of civilisation and society.'

'Sure I've heard of him. Barefoot bruiser of a guy. Me, I'm not that tough. Round here I wear sandals on rocky going.'

I'm keen to hear more about the Lark's experience of the island, about how he sometimes spends a night over there. More often in summer than in winter, he camps in a cave on the ocean side, out of sight of the mainland.

'Real quiet, the island. Just me and the ghosts.'

'Ghosts?'

'Friendly ones, mind. Maori people lived and died there a long time ago and there were whalers on the island for a few years. Hard doers. But, yeah, the island is a pearler of a place. Special, like Smooth Cone. There's energy in the rocks.'

Smooth Cone, in the Strath Taieri, was formed by the process of erosion, with a plug of volcanic boulders, more resistant than the surrounding schist, holding the high ground. A natural pyramid, the Lark once described it to me. He reckoned Smooth Cone had supernatural powers, and in his experience anyway, gravity was somehow less a hindrance there than on other hills. When he climbed Smooth Cone, he flowed up it. But then, the Lark always was a smooth mover.

'I've been wondering,' I say, 'whether Taieri Island was ever a cone itself at one time.'

'Maybe. Me, I'm always looking out for triangles in nature.'

'Why is that?'

The Lark rocks gently on his crossed legs as if pondering what to say next. Or whether to say anything at all.

'How should I put it? Imagine life and the universe as a triangle. Everything is moving steadily along, the whole caboodle. At the apex is the present, life as we know it, the pinnacle of evolution, no more than a pinpoint. The slope on the trailing side is the past, the slope on the leading side is the future. Reality is reduced to an abyss behind, an abyss in front and life teetering at the top.'

'Not much of a foothold,' I say, wrestling with the image.

The Lark is silent. Still as a Buddha figure, he is looking intently at the river slowly exhaling its brackish breath. The river cuts deeply into the sand on this side, creating a channel for the fishing boats. One is coming in now, motor growling. It has a halo of gulls in tow. I can see a man on the deck, togged up against the cold, gutting fish on a board, knife flashing. Blue cod probably, maybe a trumpeter or two. It must be good to get home after winter trips.

It is time I was on the road home, too. I tell the Lark I have been trying to get over to the island for a while and that if I do make it I will look out for his cave. In the meantime, I ask what his plans are, where he is heading. I doubt if I will get a straight answer. The Lark is not free with forwarding addresses. I try anyway.

'A lot of people have been asking after you, you know. They'd like to meet you.'

'Whaddya tell them?'

'That if they look hard enough they'll find you. It's a – '

'They might need to wing it. I take a bit of keeping up with. Tell them to look out for a friendly thermal.'

I might as well abandon this line of questioning. Free spirits do not easily submit to it, especially those that drift about farms, shearing, mustering, fencing or simply loafing. Just then our attention is drawn skywards. Two white-faced herons, leisurely in flight, are crossing to the other side of the river, heading away from us. Perhaps the passing fishing boat startled them from a roost in George's macrocarpa trees. I remember how the Lark had described them in the Strath Taieri.

'Winged people,' I say. 'Isn't that what you call them? Funny how a bird so wary of humans when it's on the ground can be so different in the air. Nonchalant almost.'

'Yeah, you see all kinds of personalities in the bird world. Timid, cheeky, fearless. Falcons are the bravehearts. They're not easily frightened.'

'Nor are sea lions, for that matter,' I venture. 'They'll stand their ground.'

The Lark pauses to consider this comment of mine. It seems I have touched a chord, perhaps a whole series of chords. It must be a merry tune, for his eyes are dancing. He asks me what I know about sea lions. I tell him I am learning what I can about them and that my interest in Taieri Mouth arose from the birth here of the first sea lion pups recorded on mainland New Zealand.

'All going well,' I add, 'I intend getting some first-hand experience with them at their breeding grounds in the Auckland Islands. A few months away. The subantarctic. Got a trip lined up with a sea lion expedition going to Enderby Island.'

'You don't say,' says the Lark. Then, 'Sea people.' His voice trails off, distant.

'I'm sorry, I didn't quite catch that.'

'Sea lions, they're sea people. Personalities. I know that mother one.'

'You mean you've seen her yourself?'

'Too true. She's pretty darned special. But you know that anyway. We've had our moments, me and her. I've said hello to one or two others besides, mainly young fellows, and one in particular. They're not thick on the ground here, and I – '. The Lark interrupts himself. He puts down his mug and adjusts his Swanni, seemingly unsure of what to say next. I fancy it is time to excuse myself, say goodbye and head back to my car when suddenly he continues with his train of thought.

'Know anything about selchies?' he asks, eyebrows lifted quizzically.

'Not much,' I say. My mind's radar is scanning for information. I get a blip. 'Only that there's some sort of Gaelic tradition behind the name. All I can think of is an Irish movie I saw at a film festival a while back. It was called "The Secret of Roan Inish" or somesuch. I have a hazy impression it portrayed a little girl's friendship with a seal. A dreamy sort of film.'

'I've not seen that one myself – don't go in much for movies. No, it was my old grandad who told me about selchies, from stories he had told to him as a lad in Scotland. A selchie is someone in a seal's body. The stories go back centuries – of men marrying seal women, of selchies saving fishermen from disaster at sea, of seals singing. Talking even. They reckoned anyone who killed a seal ran the risk of coming back in the next life as one, all weepy eyed.'

The Lark is watching me closely, judging my reactions, I guess, and wondering if he is sounding plausible. Where the Lark is concerned, I've been surprised before.

'It's all a half-baked myth, isn't it?' I say, rising to my feet and brushing the sand off my clothes. It is time I was on my way. 'Do you believe these stories?' I get no reply. 'With a bit of luck, I'll see you here in the summer?' I put my hand forward to shake his.

The Lark wants the last word. 'If we get to coincide with the sea lions I'll show you something.'

'Like what?'

'You wait and see. Bring a wetsuit.'

'See you, then.'

'Not if I spot you first'. His hand is extended. There's webbing between his robust fingers. I know we all have a bit of skin that arcs between the fingers, and the toes as well. But I swear, in the Lark's case, the webbing on his hands is more developed than you would see on most people.

FIVE

SHE DIED AT ABOUT 40 years of age, a smallish woman, just over five feet tall. Her people, coastal Maori, buried her in an unmarked shallow grave at the north end of the island – Moturata, Rata Island. We do not know her name. Nor do we know what caused her death. But to live to 40 in those times – 250 years ago, give or take a few decades – was quite an achievement. She could have died of old age. In those times – Captain Cook's era – the life expectancy in Europe, let alone this part of the world, was little better than 40. The woman's teeth were blunt from a rough tough diet, which probably included shellfish in abundance. She had borne several children. Her bones said so.

When her bones were exposed a few years ago by erosion, they were carefully and reverently collected from the crumbling clay, and later reburied in another part of the island, a place less threatened by erosion. Before the reburial, the bones were examined by an Otago Medical School anatomist who has studied Polynesian people of pre-European times. This woman's history of childbirth was written in the pitting of her pubic bone, a phenomenon common to child-bearing women everywhere, then as now. During childbirth, even perhaps before it through the release of a softening-up hormone, joint ligaments are ruptured around the pelvis and pubic bone, and the damage shows up as little craters on the bone, smoothly formed like raindrops in soft mud. The pitting on the Moturata woman was extensive, indicating she had given birth to several children.

Nothing more is known of the circumstances of her life. As for her death, did she die on the island or across the way? For how long did her people mourn? All we know is that she was laid to rest in the urupa at the island's northern tip, an ancestral burial ground. The urupa – what little remains of it, for much of it has been washed or blown away – looks out over a narrow line of wave-washed rocks extending north from the island. The urupa was a leaping-off place for the spirits of the dead. From here they had ready access to the unfathomable, incomprehensible spirit world.

When the north bar is open, outbound fishing boats pause in the lee of the urupa site and the line of rocks as if paying their respects. In a sense they are; their crews are watching the pattern of the swells, watching and waiting for a quiet moment during which they can leap off to their fishing grounds. Timing is everything.

Even to visit the island when there is no access on foot by way of the ephemeral sandspit, timing is important. You have to time it right for tide and weather, and fit in with fishing opportunities if you are relying on a fishing boat to get you there. With the aid of the Taieri Mouth fishing vessel *Kiri V*, a nine-metre crayfish and cod boat, I finally make it to the island in the company of Taieri Mouth identity Martin Palmer, who is a leading light in the local Maori community, and two staff from the Department of Conservation, which manages the island as a scenic reserve.

Martin has organised the visit. He is the nearest thing to a caretaker – kaitiaki – for the island. From his house on the slopes above Taieri Beach he keeps watch over Moturata. He can read the sea and mouth conditions as well as anyone. You could say the sea is in his blood despite his long experience of farming the land here. He is a direct descendant of the whaling Palmers. His great-grandfather, Edwin Palmer, born in 1829, journeyed to New Zealand as a boy. Edwin's uncles, Edward and William Palmer, managed whaling stations in the south in the 1830s, and William probably worked at the Taieri Island shore station at one time. Edwin, known as Ned, married into a chiefly family of Foveaux Strait Maori, and spent most of his life farming and fishing around Taieri Mouth and Henley. Martin went to the Taieri Beach School during the war years. George McIntosh was a school mate. The families would make a point of getting to the island on New Year's Day for a picnic if at all possible. Martin is steeped in the place.

Which is probably why, on this winter visit, he feels more confident than me about stepping off the *Kiri V* and into a brown current that separates us from the island. It is hard to judge the depth. It looks shallow enough. But his calf-length Red Band gumboots are swamped immediately as he tries to cross the five metres between boat and dry sand. Now he is sinking in the soft sand, and the flow, half river, half sea, is sucking him away from the boat. It is a dodgy moment. You do not mess about in a current with gumboots on. In a flash, *Kiri V*'s skipper, Graham Fraser, is at the side of the boat and offering Martin a hose pipe, the nearest thing close at hand with which to reach him. It is only just long enough. Martin is promptly hauled aboard, soaked to his thighs.

We try another approach. This time the boat's stern 'leg' is lifted clear of the bottom and we can nose right up to the sandbank, and step ashore with dry feet. Except for Martin who is sloshing about in his Red Band gumboots. No matter, he is dry up top and his trusty Swanndri, a brown check pattern, will keep him that way on land whether it rains or not. As a concession to his wet feet he removes the sodden rugby socks, wrings the water from them and, for the duration of our stay on the island, carries them flapping in his hands, hoping they will dry.

Martin's minor mishap reminds me of surveyor Frederick Tuckett's experience here. Having spent the night 'grumbling' on the beach opposite the island, he was probably in no better mood the next day when he and Dr Monro visited the whalers. 'The waves break to and fro that it seems impossible to get across without being swamped,' he wrote. Maori escorts with them refused to visit the island. Whether the Maori were dissuaded by the sacred or waahi tapu nature of the island or by Tuckett's petulance, we will never know. Finally, the whalers sent a boat, which put the surveyors on the island in 'a thunder of foam'. They found the whalers were living in 'grass huts' and in the process, that very day, of cutting up a whale.

' … nowhere, perhaps, do twenty Englishmen reside in a spot so comfortless as this naked inaccessible isle.' In massive iron bowls called trypots they rendered oil from blubber (a large whale could yield 120 barrels or 17,000 litres) for the markets of Europe and North America. The boats chased them as far as Green Island, a long way to row at speed. Generally, though, the harpooning was done closer to Taieri Island (spelt Tyree or Tyarie by the whalers), and the boat steersman took directions from a lookout on the island's high point.

Old William Palmer told how sperm whales sometimes came close to shore to scratch themselves. They would rub their sides on rocks in shallow water in an effort to scrape off barnacles. Whaling was a short-lived enterprise nonetheless. Whales, whether right whales or sperm whales, were scarce. The Weller Brothers' business collapsed in 1841. The Taieri Island station was revived in 1844 but did not survive for long. The last return recorded from Taieri Island (45 tons of oil, two tons of whalebone) was in February, 1845.

The rusted trypot of Baxter's poem is probably the one that rests, symbolically, in Martin and Barbara Palmer's front garden. On the island, a fire was lit between the three legs of the trypot, fuelled by logs of rata and other trees. No wonder Tuckett and Monro described the island as naked. Smoke belching from the trypots blackened the cliffs facing the river. The cliffs are no longer 'begrimed', but in places they have been stripped of a protective curtain of iceplant by the daily parade of blue penguins.

Promising a circumnavigation of the seven-hectare island before the *Kiri V* returns, Martin leads us up to the urupa site first, and we approach wondering whether recent storms have exposed any more bones. Erosion is relentless once it gets a hold. Introduced mallow and the native shore hebe, *Hebe elliptica*, are colonising the site, softening its rawness. On the flat area above, a small miracle is occurring. Springy mats of manuka seedlings have established – but not by chance. A revegetation project is responsible, coordinated by the kaitiaki with assistance from the Department of Conservation.

Martin had been concerned Moturata would turn into a desert island if something were not done to curb the erosion. Rabbits were eating the young seedlings and allowing southerly gales to blow away the exposed soil. The island badly needed healing.

First aid came by helicopter. Bundles of manuka branches

from the Taieri Beach area were airlifted to the island in slings dangling under the helicopter. There were dozens of loads. Volunteers spread the manuka 'slash' over the wounded land and tied down the branches with number eight fencing wire so it would not blow away. Seed arrived with the slash, and under its protective cover manuka seedlings are coming up together with grasses, herbs and shrubs. As for the rabbits, they succumbed to a poisoning programme. Martin doubts if there are any left.

The titi will miss the rabbits. Titi are sooty shearwaters, migratory sea birds that breed in their millions in the New Zealand region, especially the cooler southern islands, over summer. Their young are known as muttonbirds and routinely harvested by Maori in the autumn on islands off Stewart Island. Moturata was once a muttonbird island, too, an important resource for the people of this area in pre-European times. Titi nest in burrows, which they usually dig in sandy loam. Rabbits are more efficient diggers, though, and on Moturata they have provided the titi with holes too deep for the muttonbirders to access. 'Best friend of the muttonbird, the rabbit,' is what George McIntosh says.

The other major burrower here is the blue penguin. Titi and blue penguins use each other's holes: first come, first served. Occasionally there are boundary disputes. Wings versus flippers. Up ahead of us, beside a line of flax bushes, the sand is flying. A penguin is creating new real estate, raking its way into the bank. The webbed feet that hurl the sand so vigorously are equipped with sharp claws for cutting into the sand.

We are careful where we walk here. The ground is riddled with burrows. A boot can easily go through the roof of the shallower ones. Above the urupa site the flat land now covered by manuka branches is the site of a prehistoric fishing camp. Martin pulls back some of the slash to reveal a small quadrangle of stones, the remains of a hearth, he says. Its builders would have gathered paua and mussels from the tidal rocks on the seaward side and they would have fished there for blue cod and greenbone. Also available to them were penguin and gull eggs in summer and muttonbird fledglings in autumn. And perhaps a fur seal for additional protein. They cooked food on the island in a number of places, judging by the scattered presence of blackened cooking stones, shattered by the heat of the fire. Some of the stones, once well buried, are showing up where the soil has been washed and blown away. When the weather was rough or the tide awkward, the fishing camp was probably a place for fashioning fish hooks from bone, and ornaments or implements from the precious, much-travelled pounamu or greenstone. The little hearth is the only monument left to this enterprise.

You do not see any evidence now of the whaling station nor anything more than a few bricks from the pilot station that followed it to serve goldfields traffic on the river in the early 1860s. There were 25 men at the whaling station in its last days. Many had Maori wives, as was the custom. A visitor unacquainted with the island's history would never suspect large whales were winched ashore here, dissected, disembowelled and melted down. Martin points out a cave on the landward side where the whalers evidently collected freshwater. Water trickles off the land still. Some things never change. Nearby is a small beach where they finished off the whales and gutted them as if they were no more than oversized fish.

We are at the top of the island now, some 30 metres above sea level and surrounded by dense flax. The flax is the equivalent of a thick mop of hair. It has saved the island from being scalped by the elements. Martin created a gap at the summit last year and planted five young rata trees to try to put the rata back into Rata Island. He would like to live long enough to see them flower. 'We'll have this place back to a fairly natural condition, well clothed, in ten to fifteen years, you watch,' he says. Besides rata, he and his helpers have planted broadleaf seedlings, small-leaved coprosmas, fluffy-flowered toetoe and sand-binding pingao.

To the ocean side of the island we go now, crossing open ground where the next manuka bandaging is due to be applied. The bare soil, whale-grey, might easily have been blackened by trypot smoke instead of, as is surely the case, by plant remains. Whereas the landward side of the island has been pared smooth by sou'west gales, the ocean side has a rugged appearance, the result of pounding by waves that have dislodged and shattered the rocks.

The wild blue yonder lies west of here. Next stop, South America, no kidding. Big beyond imagining, it has a lot to say – as Baxter says, it is always talking. Where it meets the shore, it is especially vocal, and small islands like this one, bearing both soft and hard shores, offer the sea a chance to fully vent itself. You can hear its sibilant hiss on soft sand, a rasping on coarser beaches, a spluttering, gravelly voice on pebbles and a booming bass note on bluffs and stacks.

There used to be three rock arches on the landward side of the island. An earthquake on the Akatore Fault destroyed two of them some years ago. The third arch, on the ocean side, was made of stouter stuff. Martin is glad it survived. He remembers how, while out fishing, you could access a superb groper hole by lining up the archway hole with a building on the mainland. The groper have largely disappeared. Fished out, is the consensus. It would be easy enough for whole populations to crash as a result of too much fishing at their winter spawning grounds, the deeper holes. The groper is prized by Maori, who call them hapuka, as well as by pakeha fisherfolk. The daddy of them all is bass groper, which has a massive head and undershot jaw. Bass groper could reach almost two metres in length and 50 kilograms in gutted weight.

Older Maori warned fishermen not to let a hooked hapuka touch the side of the boat. If it did, you might as well head for home. The hapuka would stop biting. Perhaps vibrations from the struggle carried into the water through the hull of the boat, sending warning signals to all groper below. Upon such caveats are fishing fortunes made or lost. The Taieri Mouth fishing industry was founded in the late 1920s on line fishing for groper and blue cod. Trawling for the high-value flat fish – lemon sole, English sole, brill and flounder – began soon afterwards.

We are slowly reeling in the island, encircling it anticlockwise, getting its measure. I know who is hooked. Me. It is a wonderfully atmospheric place, with a shadowy past and a luminous future. We will soon be back where we started from: the northern end. There is one important feature we have yet to see, though. We passed a cave earlier on this ocean side, deep, dark and reeking of rotting seaweed and penguin excreta. I knew it was not what the Lark described. A group of blue penguins stood at the back in a nervous, shifty huddle, white bellies shining in the faint light. We left them to it. The second cave is more welcoming. It is not so much a cave as a generous overhang. Its ceiling penetrates over five metres into the base of the cliff. Between the pebbly floor and the ceiling is a rock shelf that slopes down to be waist high at the front. What catches one's attention immediately is an oval hollow at the edge of the shelf, a natural hand-basin. It is brimming with water that trickles down the shelf, spring fresh. But is the basin natural? Chances are, it was excavated by early Maori or by whalers as a convenient water supply.

'Holds forty-eight cups,' says Martin, noticing my interest in the basin. 'Measured it once. We had the Conservation Corps people out here helping with the reveg work. Thirsty work it was, too.'

I try the water myself. It is clear but slightly salty, tainted perhaps by salt-laden onshore winds, the redoubtable nor'easters. If you camped here overnight you could help yourself to a drink without getting out of your sleeping bag. The source of fresh water was no doubt a key reason for the long-running Maori occupation of the island.

I try stretching out on the floor. Yes, I could manage the night here if need be.

Martin is looking out to sea for a sign of the *Kiri V*. Sky and sea are both grey and lumpy and virtually seamless. Spotting an aluminium hull is not easy. We have had three hours on the island so we expect our vessel to appear any moment. We continue on to the northern end, clambering over rocks shot through with colour. I have heard that jasper occurs here, a vein of it, which might account for shades of purple, red, green and yellow. Derived from quartz, jasper polishes up as a gemstone. But some of the rocks on the island are completely out of character. They look like volcanic basalt, sandblasted smooth by the winds. Maybe they arrived in whaling vessels as ballast.

I notice that one of the rocks, grey-brown and boulder-round, is moving. It has whiskers to boot, and it utters a sharp, disconcerted snort. It is a New Zealand fur seal, a very large male. It lifts its head from a snoozing position at the sound of boots rattling rocks. Its fur is dry and bristly, and it looks ready to bolt for the sea. Bull seals not guarding harems in the breeding season invariably take fright at the approach of humans. In this case the animal is probably close to twice my weight, is equipped with a scary set of teeth and could negotiate the boulders as easily as I could; yet he is terrified. There is dread in his bulging eyes. How come? Is the fear embedded in his genes? Do New Zealand fur seals as a race carry ancestral memories of the killing time, when gangs of men came in sailing ships with knives and clubs to redden the shallows? The slaughter was widespread; it was mass destruction.

No seal populations were safe in southern New Zealand.

Given the skittery nature of fur seals today, it is difficult to imagine how the sealing gangs of the early 1800s managed to exterminate them so rapidly from most areas, even if their assaults coincided with the breeding season when the harem bulls would stand their ground. You have to ask yourself: were the fur seals a more confiding race before the sealers came?

The Moturata bull scrambles away on frenzied flippers. Once in the water, though, and nosing around the fronds of bull kelp in a gut in the tidal rocks, he seems transformed – a creature in his element, distinctly unrattled. The sea is his security blanket. It figures. He knows – I am sure he does – that I will not follow him.

The *Kiri V* returns. One minute the sea is empty; the next there is a grey hull belting through the swells close enough for us to identify her. We climb down the low cliffs and get ready to wade out over the shelving sand on the island's lee side, which is in the process of being flooded by the incoming tide. As he guns the *Kiri V* back up the river to the jetties I tell Graham about the bull seal. I ask him if he has ever seen sea lions here. Only very occasionally, he says. But he does remember one encounter.

'Hell, must be thirty years ago,' he says. 'A sea lion hauled out on the sand at the island. Couple of guys thought they'd have a crack at it. They got dropped off with clubs and a gaff. Next thing, the animal is charging at them and they jump back on the boat quick as look.'

It's a sobering story. Come early spring, I expect to be confronting sea lions close up myself, at subantarctic Enderby Island. No club or gaff for us. From what the scientists running the project tell me, we'll be capturing sea lions alive in a heavy net and wrestling them to a standstill. It is a peculiar kind of hands-on work.

Enderby is to Moturata what Moturata is to the little island at

Brighton – bigger and wilder. All three have a history of Maori settlement, and Enderby and Moturata share an association with whaling and old-time seafaring. But Enderby is much less modified by humans. It is the lair of the New Zealand sea lion. It is a sea lion breeding centre, a leaping-off place.

PART II

Enderby

> *'Web-footed seals forsake the stormy swell,*
> *and sleep in herds, exhaling nauseous smell ...'*
>
> HOMER, circa 800 BC

ONE

NOT ONE FOR SNOOZING long, the beachmaster raises himself up on his broad front flippers and gazes seawards, alert in a lumbering sort of way. Four hundred kilograms is a big weight to lift at short notice. His muzzle is tipped upwards, imperiously, suspiciously. He sniffs the air. His mouth opens to reveal two fearsome tapering pegs that are his lower canine teeth, one on each side of the jaw. His right cheek is a mess of scar tissue. Two years ago, while fishing in a school of squid that was also the target of a squid-jigging vessel, he ran into a multi-barbed jigger hook, a miniature grappling iron. It ripped an ugly hole in his cheek. When he yawns, the inside of his mouth is visible through the hole. Sand picked up while snoozing clings to the brown facial hair, giving him a grey-bearded look that complements the silver tinge of his dry, fluffed-up mane. His mane is a mark of his maturity. He is 12 years old, and this is his second season as a beachmaster. He might have two more years as a breeding bull, with a territory and females to guard, then he is likely to be deposed in a bloody no-holds-barred clash with one of the younger bulls now patrolling the shoreline. Above one eye he bears the scar of a deep wound inflicted by a pretender to his throne last summer. He beat off the challenger, just.

Position is everything for a male New Zealand sea lion, known also as Hooker's sea lion, in the breeding season. At Sandy Bay on Enderby Island, from late November, the biggest, strongest and most experienced bulls stake out a patch of creamy sand, each to his own patch. There is an atmosphere of mutual distrust. Made aggressive by the male hormone testosterone that surges through their bloodstream at this time of year, they defend their patch not only till the cows come home but also till they give birth and are once more ready for mating. The cows come home in December. They are heavily pregnant; they must give birth soon.

The scar-faced beachmaster surveys his patch of sand with dark liquid eyes – dark as the ocean deep. Something has roused him on this sunny morning. Probably it was a commotion at the water's edge directly down the beach from him, where a female, newly arrived from sea, is trying to avoid the noisy ambush of one of the young pretender bulls. They think they can herd and corner females at the tide line. They have no chance. The sleek females, known also as sea bears, are bound to join a beachmaster's territory, as has always been the way, because they want to settle well up on the beach. All the beachmaster can do is establish a territory in the expectation of females ending up there. He has no more say in the matter than that. It is up to the cows to choose where they will end up on the beach. A beachmaster may find his patch crowded with a dozen or more cows or he may have to plump for just a couple. For him, breeding time is a bit of a lottery. By definition, though, he will be among the ablest of the bulls of that season. Only the superior males get to pass on their genes.

Scarface emits a low-frequency rumble as the newly arrived cow tries to skirt around the young male. She sidesteps and dodges, bending her neck almost 180 degrees to fend him off with a hoarse, open-mouthed bellow. He, in turn, jabs at her rear end, appearing ready to bite. But he does not bite. As he knows this time, and so many other times, the game is lost. The cow scampers on up the beach into the midst of Scarface's ladies, numbering nine already. Beside his dark brutish form, the cows are golden, sleek and somnambulant on the sand. They lie closely packed because they like it that way – they like the touch and the company – and also because their beachmaster herds them into a tight formation. The more closely packed they are, the more manageable.

Scarface acknowledges the addition to his harem by shuffling over to her, scattering some of his other females in the process. He noses her rear. He would not choose to leave his station to rescue her from the suitor at the water's edge. He might be overthrown if he did. His patch is sacrosanct only while he attends it. He can stretch the boundaries a metre or two at a time and perhaps lasso a neighbour's cow but he must always weigh up whether it is worth a battle royal to extend his territory.

A quick sniff tells him the newcomer has yet to deliver her pup. Her reaction is to roar in his face and lunge at his well-padded chest. In reply the beachmaster produces a thunderous outpouring of breath. They have traded scents. There is now an uneasy understanding between them, beachmaster and sea bear. He returns to his regular station and for a time remains up on his haunches, watchful from his throne.

Then, as if mindful of his status and the need to keep up appearances, he begins to groom himself. Grooming or scratching involves lifting and swivelling a flipper, front flipper or a hind one, and deftly stroking an area of fur with rudimentary nails – a curiously gentle action for such a large and at times unruly animal. The nails are a quaint sign of the sea lion's ancient origins as a land animal. Sea lions have evolved from bear-like carnivores that 30 million years ago began sampling and exploring the intertidal zone. Gradually, they adapted to a life at sea. Although their nails still sprout from the end of digital bones, they are overlapped by leathery flaps of skin, especially on the hind flippers where only the middle three of the five nails have survived the adaptation. Between the digits, webbed skin developed. Thus did paws become flippers. All sea lions and seals belong to a family called pinnipeds – wing-footed ones.

At Sandy Bay the day has warmed to an uncomfortable 15 degrees Celsius. For the beachmaster there is no escaping the heat and glare of the sun. A cooling dip in the subantarctic sea is out of the question. His only reprieve from the heat is to hunker down, flick sand over himself with one or both front flippers and lazily extend a flipper into the air to catch any breeze going. The creamy sand will reflect some of the sun's heat. Through the warmest part of the day, coated in sand, he keeps his chin flat on the sand and his eyes closed. But other senses are still on guard. His furry earflaps, ridiculously petite on a head so large, flicker briefly in a reflex sort of way. And his whiskers twitch. Drooping gaucho-like from both sides of his snout, the thick sparse hairs or vibrissae form part of his sensory apparatus. In the open air he can feel temperature changes through them; in water they perform other miracles.

Perhaps that is what he is dreaming now – of bathing his whiskers in cool sea water, letting them sound out shapes beyond his visual range, shapes such as schools of fish, other sea lions or the undulating seabed. Jam-packed with nerve fibres, his whiskers help tune him in to the underwater world. For the moment he can only dream of such things. He is sentenced to a brawling foodless life ashore for two months, all for the sake of passing on his genes. And to accomplish that he must wait for each cow to pup and come into heat a week after the pup's arrival.

TWO

BETWEEN THE DEMENTED screechings of a gang of skuas comes a plaintive, lonesome cry. It carries through the cool, grey dawn at Sandy Bay, sounding not quite like a lamb or baby goat but something between the two: a lament in any mammalian language. The bleating increases as the fat-bellied skuas go about their bloody business, tearing at a freshly delivered placenta. Half hawk, half gull, the skuas behave as marauding camp followers at sea lion breeding time: the sea lion city's loyal, if noisy, cleansing staff. They tear at and devour placentas, and pups still-born or weak. Although they possess a hawk's hooked bill, skuas lack a raptor's talons to do the job efficiently. Their feet are webbed like those of a black-backed gull. To dismember prey they work co-operatively, pulling in opposite directions in a frenzy of flapping wings, high-pitched shrieks and flying sand. But while it demonstrates vitality and has its mother alongside, a new-born pup is not in any danger of succumbing to the skuas. On the contrary, a skua scrambling too close might suffer a broken wing – and ensuing death – from a sea bear's lunging bite.

There goes that cry again, rising and croakily falling away. It speaks of something vulnerable and too young to be left alone. It speaks also of fear and craving: fear of the shadowy hulking forms nearby that could snuff out the life of the pup simply by rolling the wrong way, and craving for that which only mother can deliver – milk and the comfort of her smell and touch.

The pup's first instinct is to verify its identity and the centre of its universe. On shaky limbs, it wriggles and staggers through the lumpy sand towards the head of the sea bear, whose experience of the overnight birth has left her needing to doze as day breaks. There were no complications; there rarely are. Less than ten minutes after the membranes of the chorionic sac ruptured, the pup, a male, came sliding out headfirst in two movements, seconds apart – a shiny, slippery bag, with no collar bone or shoulders to snag in the birth canal. A smooth exit from the uterus is also assisted by the mother's slender pelvis. Having relatively weak hind limbs, sea lions, like all seals, do not require the pelvic bone development typical of many terrestrial animals so the birth canal is not impeded by a heavy pelvis. As the pup's head emerged, face down, the sea bear jerked her rear end sideways to help expel the new-born, a movement that broke the umbilical chord. Then she doubled over to sniff and lick the dark wet bag. Its scent she would never forget. Half an hour later the placenta emerged, and three waiting skua closed on it in a flash, tearing at the limp red parcel. They can demolish a four kilogram placenta in under half a minute.

Like all new-borns, male or female, the sea bear's pup is brown overall when he dries out, with a buff stripe running down the top of his snout and around it and dark fur surrounding his eyes – a comic sort of mask. His snout is marginally blunter and more robust than that of a female pup. He uses it now to request his first need, nudging the midriff of the sea bear. The mother's response is to roll half over, waving one foreflipper in the air. There is room for this manoeuvre among the harem because she has moved slightly apart from the other females to give birth. The pup pokes about on the pale underside. Although his eyes have been open since birth, he is directed more by touch and smell than by sight. He mistakes a black spot for a nipple then finds the real thing. There are four teats, each of which delivers an oily milk five times as rich as cow's milk. The mammary tissue on sea lions, in two sections, is spread flat across the belly to preserve the streamlined shape of the animal for efficient swimming and diving. Even at the peak of lactation the glands and nipples lie flat. Unlike cow's milk and that of humans, there is little lactose or sugar in sea lion milk, and little water. Protein content is high at over 10 percent. The pup sucks softly and creamy milk spills from the side of his mouth. The wrinkly bag has begun filling up. Mother and pup are bonded. But it is a bond that will depend on lactation. Sea lions do not maintain family groups in the way that whales and dolphins do. Once weaned, later in the year, he will be on his own.

On his second day the pup is baptised into the hurly-burly of sea lion breeding. A female in the same group, yet to give birth, acts as if the pup is hers. She drags him towards her, gently at first then with some urgency as his mother suddenly senses an abduction occurring. The sea bear roars, lunges, and grasps her pup in her jaws. A tug of love ensues, with the would-be abductor clamping on to the pup's hindflippers and mother holding him around the neck in her jaws. The sea bear wins out. A pitiful whimper rises from the pup. He lies slumped on the sand, too stunned even to seek solace at a nipple. He must face sterner tests yet.

The Sandy Bay colony is reaching a peak of activity as Christmas approaches. Pups are arriving in number now, and their appearance spurs the beachmaster bulls into more aggressive defence of their territories. A week after giving birth, females come into heat. All the fighting and fasting on the part of the bulls has positioned them for the moment of oestrus. They must seize the moment. Oestrus lasts just a few days. Meanwhile, the shore bulls, desperate to strut their stuff, continue to ambush the late-arriving females and the mated ones heading back to the water to feed.

The sea bear's beachmaster has been checking out her condition since the appearance of her pup on his patch. As the days tick over he visits her more often, sniffing her rear end for the arousing scent of fertility. Towards the end of the week there is a pronounced gruffness about his behaviour towards her, expressed in his voice, half cough, half roar. He has a job to do. He is boss of this patch.

On finding her in heat one day, he wastes no time. Other females in the group make space on the sand as he lays a foreflipper on her back and shuffles his hind quarters more in line with hers. The sea bear is prone and pressed deeply into the soft sand. Other than raise and turn her head a little, she makes no attempt to avoid his approaches, and makes no sound. Copulation lasts less than a minute. She is pinned underneath him the whole time but the beachmaster takes at least some of his great weight on his foreflippers, which straddle her. While thrusting with his hindquarters, he holds his head high and stoically. His head turns slowly one way then the other, a radar on alert for any rival bull that might use this opportunity to make inroads on his patch. When the sea bear has had enough, she lets him know. She thrashes her upper body and swivels her head to bite at his massive chest. He gets the message and backs off submissively. He will try to impregnate her again later in the day.

Within the sea bear's reproductive organs, an egg awaits the arrival of a fertilising sperm. The egg has come from the ovary opposite to that which produced this year's pup. Fertilised, the egg will become a blastocyst. It will float in the uterus, growing slowly to the size of a pinhead. Then it will enter a state of suspended growth, known as embryonic diapause, until the walls of the uterus are ready to accept it, some three months into the new year. In common with most mammals, the foetus puts on most of its growth in the last three months. Timing is everything. The sea lions of Enderby Island and elsewhere in the Auckland

Islands hold to a tight breeding timetable in the middle of the subantarctic summer.

Newly mated, the sea bear feels the need to feed again. She needs to feed for the sake of her milk supply. After herding her pup into a pod of new-borns at the edge of the beachmaster's territory, she eyes up the quiet waters of Sandy Bay, the outer reaches of Port Ross, then makes a run towards the shore. The beachmaster sees her go but is unmoved. The bulls patrolling the shore are not so complacent. Eager-beavers, ready to serve any female that hesitates, they try to block the sea bear's egress. She gets turned back in the low surf, where the water boils with the cut and thrust of the ambush, and she has to retreat back up the beach. In a few moments she tries a new angle through the blubbery gauntlet. This time she escapes, mainly because she is more agile in the shallows than the bulky males. Once in deeper water she becomes a torpedo.

THREE

LIKE GAMBOLLING LAMBS, the pups grouped between beachmaster territories amuse themselves throughout the day, running at each other, tossing and shaking sticks, shells and bits of seaweed, and mock fighting. They sink their milk teeth into the furry necks of other pups, imitating the sparring bulls. The sea bear's pup is one of the bolder ones in his group, and already an adventurous fellow. During his mother's absences he has tried stealing milk from females yet to pup and even from mothers with pups handy. Mostly he is shoved on but milk-filching does pay off at times.

During one such excursion, he stumbled into a fight between his beachmaster and the nextdoor neighbour. It nearly cost him his life. At the end of the clash, which left a sliver of pearly-white fat exposed on the neck of his beachmaster, the enormous animal parked himself on the pup, oblivious to the pup's pained shrieks. If the beachmaster had rolled a few centimetres further he would have squashed the breath right out of the pup. Only a challenge to the beachmaster from another direction, which forced him into a retaliatory move, saved the pup. After that close call, the pup was sore and subdued, and he bleated for his mother. Rain came instead. It spilled from a thunderously dark sky as a westerly gale churned the waters in Port Ross, most northerly harbour of the Auckland Islands. The pup blinked at the angled rain, and found some cooling comfort in it after two days of bright sunshine.

When the sea bear returns late the next day, she walks purposefully up the beach, calling to her pup. She goes directly to where she left him. She sniffs at several pups in the vicinity but recognises none of them. She finally locates him where the sand meets a low grassy bank – the edge of a sloping sward between beach and rata forest. Even though his call and appearance mark him out from the other pups, his scent is the main identifying feature. The sea bear sniffs his face and licks him to back up the impression. She flops on the sand, showing the nipples on her pale underside, and the pup needs no second prompt. He drinks his fill of milk and comfort. Mum is home for a day or two.

January is more than half gone. Nights remain short – just five hours long – but they are lengthening slowly nonetheless. The sea bear senses her pup is ready to explore beyond the beach so she leads him up the bank at the back and on to the grass sward. Whereas she walks on braced flippers as most four-legged animals do, moving diagonally opposite limbs at the same time, the pup has a scrambly gait and he climbs the lip of the bank with a flurry of flipper strokes. The grass is a texture new to him. He sniffs it, and plucks at it with his mouth but is not tempted to eat it.

Within a quarter of an hour of introducing him to the sward, the sea bear leaves again for sea and another offshore foraging excursion. Her pup is engrossed in his new surroundings. There is so much more room here, not to mention new experiences. He ambles over to a bare patch in the grass to find another pup staring bleakly out at him from a hole – an old rabbit hole, dating from the days when Enderby Island supported hundreds of French blue-grey rabbits. He sniffs the pup in the hole, perhaps hoping it will come out and play. But it cannot move its flippers. If it cannot extract itself it will slowly die of starvation.

Farther on, the exploring pup finds a bog hole and the remains of a pup, bloated with eyes plucked. As he leans over the edge of the hole, alerted by the stench that all is not well here, a noisy cloud of blowflies rises from the carcass.

Splashing sounds catch his attention. Towards the edge of the sward several pups are playing in a small stream. The newcomer joins them, sniffing the water before walking into it. He jerks his head, dog-like, to flick water from his whiskers then dips his snout in. The water is dark and quick-flowing. In a small pool, he pushes his head under to discover a new marvel: if he opens his eyes underwater he can see.

Later in the day he returns to the beach in case his mother should return – and to sleep on the cushioning sand. His mother does not come. In the evening, before dusk comes coolly creeping over Enderby Island, he resorts to play-fighting with other pups. Their activity attracts a black-faced adolescent male sea lion. At four years of age, the sub-adult male (Sam) is too young and underdeveloped to challenge a shore bull, let alone a beachmaster, but his hormones are already beginning to bother him. He arrives among the pups roaring. With no mothers in sight – most are at sea feeding – he means business. He starts herding the pups as if this patch of sand is his territory and the pups are his females. He rushes towards a pup trying to escape, grabs it by the back of the neck and flings it into the group. Next, hellbent on buggery, he tries to copulate with the pup. Any pup will do, male or female. He is not selective. The assaulted pup must carry Sam's buffeting weight. Some pups die on the spot for the sake of this pubescent training, and some suffer a damaged flipper or crushed internal organs.

As darkness arrives the adolescent stops the torment, and the pups without mothers go to sleep slumped on the sand and in places stacked two-deep for comfort. The night is never completely quiet, however. Somewhere in the colony there is minor mayhem or mating or both.

The morning brings an altogether new experience. Two tall creatures are moving slowly through the colony, pausing where there are pods of pups. They are gluing white plastic patches to the heads of the newest pups. As they do not appear to be a threat, the sea bear's pup saunters up to one of the creatures, sniffing his brightly-coloured windproof clothing. It is his first smell of man. The pup jerks his head back, unsure what to think of the smell. The man slowly extends the back of his hand. Again the pup noses forward, feeling the hairs of his hand and warmth coming from it. The man turns away and continues with his work with the white patches. The sea bear's pup is not one chosen to receive a patch. In earlier years, every pup born at Sandy Bay was tagged. Plastic yellow tags, about the size of a two-dollar coin, were secured by a special tagging gun to the flap of skin in the 'armpit' of the right foreflipper. The tag was placed flush with the back edge in order to minimise piercing and avoid snagging on objects. Each tag was notched and holed in a pattern indicating the year of birth. It also carried a four-digit number that identified the individual animal. The sea bear carries such a yellow tag from her time as a pup on this beach.

Towards the end of January, the beachmasters' dominance

wanes. Mating is all but over. The pretender bulls seize the chance to challenge the half-starved beachmasters while the latter are not only losing interest but also strength. The clashes are warm-ups for next season's territorial fighting. Shore bull and beachmaster line up like Sumo wrestlers, pushing with their broad chests, mouths open and fiercely red. During pauses they seem almost embarrassed to be facing each other so closely. Wide-eyed and with whiskers almost touching, they each wait for the other to make the first move – typically a lunge at one of the front foreflippers. It is a bull's most vulnerable area. A bull with a badly torn foreflipper can be out of action for days. This lunge and counter-lunge can go on for a quarter of an hour, growing more mechanical towards the end of the contest, until one of the combatants retreats injured or withdraws out of deference to a mightier force. Wounded bulls generally recover quickly. Wounds to the chest area are often not as serious as they look. A wounded bull will not attempt to lick the injured spot. Instead he leaves the dripping dark red blood to clot, and tolerates blowflies laying eggs in or around the wound. The cheekier young bulls are now running rampant through the groups of females and pups as beachmaster authority crumbles. The party may be all but over but that does not stop the young stayers from kicking up their heels.

The sea bear's pup survives the bull mêlées. Thanks to regular suckling, he has doubled his birth weight by the end of January. His mother is about to put him to his sternest test. The sea.

FOUR

RETURNING FROM THE SEA one fine afternoon, glistening after two days foraging on the ocean floor, 30 kilometres northeast of the island, the sea bear finds her pup slumped on the sand, fast asleep. He rouses when she sniffs and prods him, and he swings around to help himself to his mobile milk bar. But instead of lying back compliantly, the sea bear begins backing towards the water. There is a clear path to the sea. Her beachmaster is stretched out on the sand, becalmed, some metres off, and most of the other females are at sea. The pup's little ears flicker as if to signal his interest in a feed. Still his mother backs away from him.

Now she is standing in the shallows, with the last line of surf slapping at her foreflippers. He waddles forward, more slowly now. As the white froth reaches his flippers he jumps back, like a cat that has dabbled a paw in a fish pond and thought better of it. But unlike the cat, the sea lion pup tentatively wades in again, hungry but uncertain. His mother bawls reassurance and he replies with a plaintive high-pitched 'Aaahh!'.

At Sandy Bay the water grows deep quickly. The pup launches himself but is no sooner afloat than he is back on the hard sand again, swept ashore by a wave. Meanwhile, the sea bear has allowed the tidal current to sweep her slowly eastward. Now the pup charges along the shoreline to keep in close contact with her and is suddenly afloat again. For half a minute he keeps his head above water and calls constantly. A bigger wave immerses him, head and all. He is swimming but without the smooth coordination of his mother. If this is his element, he has much to learn. Mother and pup swim around on the surface for a few minutes just outside the line of surf. At one point the pup, becoming tired or anxious or both, tries to climb on the sea bear's back. Then she leads him ashore, satisfied with this first swimming lesson. Milk – fatty, warm and generous – is his reward.

Towards nightfall, with the afternoon breeze having died away in the long subantarctic evening and the surf at Sandy Bay no more than a languid lick, mother and pup return to the sea. This time the sea bear swims farther out. She has to entice him with calls again but he soon follows. Head out of water, he moves with surprising speed. Suddenly his mother is no longer in view. He dips his head below the surface and there she is, performing barrel rolls, somersaulting and darting this way and that.

Next morning, the pup finds himself alone again. He wanders down to the water, tastes it, but does not venture in. Emboldened by his swimming lessons nonetheless, he walks west along the beach to a cliff-backed rocky reef that lies exposed at low tide. Within the reef are holes that pond water at low tide and a seaweed-choked gut open to the sea. He joins several other pups splashing about in one of the pools. They tug at lacy fronds of seaweed and swim in small circles. One pup, plunging his head in the water, comes up with a small crab, two legs of which he crunches before dropping it. The sea bear's pup decides to explore further. He reaches the gut, where the water gently lifts and falls in rhythm with the surges in the bay, making the skirts of bull kelp dance on the surface. To the pup this seems like a fun place but he mistakes the floating fronds of kelp for something harder and drier. From the edge of the rock platform he reaches down to test the kelp. Too late he realises it will not support his weight. He overbalances, bellyflops and experiences a few panicky moments as he thrashes his way clear of the slippery grip of the bull kelp. In the middle of the gut now but swimming freely, he turns towards the shore. The gut leads to a narrow boulder beach tucked under a dark overhang in the cliff. On his way in he disturbs two creatures he has not seen before – a pair of Auckland Island teal that were feeding on the kelp flies and other shoreline insects. Although flightless, the teal are expert at manoeuvring across the kelp. They slip quietly out of the path of the pup. Slithering and slipping, he hauls himself out on to the wet boulders.

For a minute or two he sits back on his haunches, panting more from panic than exertion. Then his thoughts turn to his belly. He sets off across the reef to return to the beach and, he hopes, mother's milk.

A week passes. He is fed three more times and swims to just beyond the surf zone every day his mother is based at Sandy Bay. His ability in the water grows with each session. It needs to. The summer is over. The autumn sunlight casts longer shadows, and the sea bear knows it is time to be moving her pup to a bush setting.

To the little one, the journey to a new home starts out like any other swim off the beach but before he knows it he has followed his mother right out of the bay. He does not look back. After surface swimming about two kilometres east along Enderby Island's rocky southern shore, mother and pup land at a place the sea bear knows of old. It is the gateway to a new kind of nursery.

Passing a few other hauled-out sea lions, mostly females with young ones, the sea bear leads her pup through a maze of large boulders covered in white and yellow lichens. At times the pup slips backwards, unable to negotiate the rocks as well as his mother, and she has to turn and nudge him into continuing. He has never climbed as far or as high before. The trail leads across a narrow band of coastal turf then on through tall dense tussocks. Mother and pup disturb a young male sea lion dozing in the grassland. He leaps up bellowing. The sea bear reacts in turn, wheeling to meet the male's charge. She positions herself between the pup and the male. They exchange breath, which fogs in the autumn air. An angry moment subsides, and mother and pup push on through a shrubland belt. The shrubs here are compact, curiously rounded and not dissimilar in colour to the dry fur of a sub-adult male sea lion. They form a zone between the tussocks and a forest of southern rata, which was ablaze with crimson flowers when the pup was a pod dweller on the sand. The forest interior is open under a tight canopy, and is kept open by sea lion trampling, generation after generation.

The sea bear and her pup have reached their destination – a small dark lake surrounded by rata forest. The sea bear brought her pup of the previous year here. Her new pup leans over the bank, sees his reflection in the still water then tastes it. He recognises fresh water. It is similar to that of the stream at Sandy Bay. But this water is much deeper. Several pups are frolicking in the lake, mock-fighting at the surface and chasing each other. At intervals they disappear in a trail of bubbles. Encouraged by these antics, the sea bear's pup jumps in. The lake is a play pool and over the next few weeks, sometimes with mother watching and sometimes without her close by, he will gain strength and skill at swimming and diving.

FIVE

IT IS APRIL. The sea bear's coat is patchy and tattered in places. She is moulting but still able to go to sea. Her pup is bulging fat. Although he spends most of his time ashore, resting in the shrubland near the lake, he has been to sea a few times in the company of his mother and watched her poke among the rocks on the sea floor close to the island for octopuses, crabs and small fish. He tries foraging himself, awkwardly. He will be a novice at it for some months yet.

Snoozing on a bed of moss at the edge of the rata forest one day while his mother is at sea, he is suddenly aware of unfamiliar sounds and lifts his head to look around. The sounds are not of sea lion nor skua nor the busy chattering parakeets that grub for food in the mossy banks and leaf litter. The pup sees enough to know that the brightly-coloured tall creatures are back and in greater numbers. He hears their murmuring and sees one of them wielding a large black floppy object. It flies through the air. The tall creatures are leaping about. The pup hears the snorting of a sea lion but cannot clearly see what is going on because of intervening trees and shrubs. At a younger age he might have gone over to investigate; this time he merely returns to his snoozing. The commotion is 20 metres away. Nothing to worry about.

For several more months yet he will live a halcyon life, sleeping, feeding from mum, going on short foraging trips with her, and playing in the lake. Come spring he will try foraging by himself in inshore waters, although he will still look out for his mother ashore and suckle from her. A day of reckoning will come in late spring. His mother will disappear. He will wait and wait for her. In the end, driven by hunger, he will have to resort to foraging alone. Meanwhile, with a new pup growing inside her, the sea bear will be a free spirit in the sea.

PART III

Going South

This place I should suppose abounds with seals, and sorry am I that the time and the lumbered state of my ship do not allow me to examine.

ABRAHAM BRISTOW,
Discoverer of the Auckland Islands, 18 August 1806

ONE

WE HAVE HAD ENDERBY ISLAND – and the high ground of the main island beyond it – in view since daybreak. Under sail and reaching across a stiff south-west wind, the 'buck-eye' ketch *Breaksea Girl* leans and punches her way through a moderate sea near the end of a 35 hour trip direct from Bluff. It is a moment to treasure, an insight into seafaring of old in the subantarctic. Sails tight-hauled and humming. Waves rearing and cresting. Seaspray cold in your face. These are the latitudes of the West Wind Drift – the Furious Fifties and Roaring Forties, the albatross latitudes. Here you can experience deep-water sailing at its gutsiest – except that in our case and for most of the way we have been chugging along under diesel power, confident of landfall at the Auckland Islands before breakfast on the second day.

Somewhere about here, also in spring but 190 years earlier, the whaler Abraham Bristow, in command of the British whaling vessel *Ocean*, sighted these islands and named them after a family friend, the first Baron Auckland. Bound for Cape Horn out of Tasmania, Bristow noted the probability of a 'good harbour in the north end' and promptly sailed on by. Not so the 21m-long *Breaksea Girl*. She is under charter to deliver us to Bristow's harbour, now known as Port Ross, and put us ashore at Enderby Island. What would the old whaler have thought about how we navigated our way here? We came courtesy not of his guiding stars but of a spacecraft: a navigation satellite.

Having welcomed the expeditionaries aboard at Bluff, owner-skipper Lance Shaw cast off, fed into the navigation system the coordinates for Port Ross and let the autopilot do the rest – well, almost. We set off in darkness, with the navigation screen showing one illuminated straight line representing the course and another running closely parallel to it, mimicking the vessel's track. On the bridge there are no roared commands of 'Port ten!' or 'Starboard five!' from the officer of the watch to whoever is on the helm. All you hear is a two-note murmur from the autopilot mechanism as, fed by signals from the satellite, it makes course corrections corresponding to the prescribed course – music to a helmsman's ears. With each soft buzzing note, a light blinks on the small black box of the autopilot – red for port, green for starboard – and the wheel twitches unaided. There is always someone on watch, of course, and our bearded skipper, looking less concerned than the night before, takes over from the watchkeeper now as we approach the fabled Auckland Islands with porridge about to go on the gimballed stove.

The seaway gradually loses its pounding energy as we enter

the lee of Enderby. Motoring now, we give the island's northeast reefs a wide berth before turning to face the sou'wester and, with speed reduced, run on into the generous mouth of Port Ross. What happens next no one would have predicted. A whale spouts a kilometre ahead of us, then another plume of water vapour appears in the characteristic V-shape of southern right whales. Moments later one of the whales breaches as if, porpoise like, it decides it should show us the way. Again and again, perhaps six times, the whale leaps, a bulky black shape against the white-capped dark-blue water of Port Ross. Although it manages to lift only about two-thirds of its chunky body clear of the water, each breach is accompanied by an enormous splash. Both whales are moving away from us at about the speed of the *Breaksea Girl* and we lose sight of them after turning towards Sandy Bay and a breakfast quietly at anchor.

Last time I was here I had only seconds to absorb the scene. I was aboard a four-engined Air Force Orion aircraft on deep-sea fisheries patrol. The Department of Conservation wanted to know whether it would be feasible to monitor seabird and seal colonies by means of aerial photography. We zoomed over Sandy Bay in January when the coastal forest blushed with flowering rata and sea lions lay dotted along the beach. It looked like something out of a glossy Club Med brochure – a sheltered bay filled with turquoise water and backed by an arc of sun-drenched golden sand. Alongside lay a green sward fit for golfing, fringed by a forest laden with crimson flowers. To the north of the island, the southern ocean appeared again, navy blue.

The view from the dining table of *Breaksea Girl* is no less inviting. Is this the subantarctic? It looks more like a shirtsleeves-and-shorts holiday spot for Bay of Islands boaties. One little wave is lolling on to the beach. I can just make out without binoculars small groups of yellow-eyed penguins either walking down from the forest or standing on a rock platform beside the water, pondering the start of another day's fishing. Two giant petrels wheel over the bay and join a posse of them on the sand at the far end of the beach. Vulture-like, they appear to be conferring about what to hunt for next. The dark motionless blobs bunched midway along the beach are male sea lions, looking decidedly off-duty. The natives certainly appear friendly.

At the edge of the forest above the western end of the beach a couple of huts stand out – our base for the next few days. Out to the left are the low-slung cliffs of Enderby, built of lava that cooled at precisely the right temperature to form basalt columns. The columns, now dressed with lichens, present a combed pattern from a distance, like vertical Venetian blinds. Or the baleen of right whales.

People lived and died for baleen in this part of the world. They came here to harvest baleen, also called whalebone, whale oil and seal skins. They were a long way from home.

The Aucklands Islands, at latitude 50 degrees south, 460 kilometres south of Bluff, 50 kilometres long and up to 27 kilometres wide, are by far the largest of New Zealand's five far-flung subantarctic island groups. East and west of here is nothing but world-encircling sea, storm-tossed much of the time. Since Bristow there have been waves of human endeavour, involving a lot of agony and precious little ecstasy. Besides whalers there were sealers, naval explorers, Maori settlers, a short-lived British settlement, castaways, sheep farmers, treasure hunters and war-time coastwatchers. They constitute layer upon layer of human drama and endeavour, the stuff of which forms legends. Uninhabited now, the Auckland Islands have become the domain of eco-tourists, scientists and conservationists, all of whom are required to tread lightly. Those well-versed in Auckland Islands history approach with a sense of awe.

We unrig a Zodiac dinghy from the stern of the vessel and

motor ashore with provisions for a week and a perplexing pile of equipment. There are three of us. Department of Conservation sea lion scientists Nick Gales and Simon Childerhouse are running the show. I have come along to lend a hand with the research work. I have come prepared. Among other things, I am toting a new pair of Red Band gumboots, a pair of state-of-the-art Seal Skinz socks (guaranteed to keep your feet dry, can you believe?), a Milair raincoat to combat the legendary driving rain, a full kit of thermal clothing, and a bottle of Buckley's Canadiol Mixture, which is an age-old remedy for colds, whose howling-wind radio advertisements made an impression on me as a youngster. Oh yes, and I packed a supply of 'Paihia Bombs', anti-seasickness tablets from a pharmacy in the Bay of Islands. They worked a treat. I was on deck or playing cards each day and half the night on the voyage from Bluff.

In millpond conditions, overheating in our thermals, we land the gear on the penguins' rock platform. Conveniently slicing through the reef is a channel lined with kelp. Simon and I lug the gear over to the beach and on up the slope to the huts while Nick gets another load before running the Zodiac on to the beach and pulling it well clear of high tide. It is warm work. We envisage a week at Enderby Island. Is this the Riviera of the Subantarctic?

Enderby, at the northern end of the group, is one of four islands that form the entrance to Port Ross. Being apart from the hilly main Auckland Island, Enderby is the 'Banana Belt' of the group – sunnier and drier.

The first task ashore is to rig the hut-based radio for communication with *Breaksea Girl* and other marine stations. Our motor ketch is departing soon for Campbell Island, two degrees of latitude farther south, to offload a team of albatross researchers, then she will return to pick us up. Nick and Simon are old hands at this sort of work. Nick, an Australian vet with a PhD from studying

Australian sea lions, is making his sixth trip. Back in Wellington he lives with his family on a yacht moored at the capital's marina. Sea air suits him. He has boyish good looks and a thick mop of wavy brown hair. Simon, younger and pony-tailed, is on his third trip here and shaping up to do a PhD.

A fire in the main accommodation hut put paid to Nick's first research visit. There are two new huts now – a kitchen/dining hut and a bunkroom – and fire extinguishers are prominently deployed. We settle in, sort gear, fix an early lunch, and walk to work. I can still feel the heaving motion of the *Breaksea Girl*. It is a day for sun screen, sunglasses and lip salve. What would the castaways have thought?

Work is about two kilometres away on the coastal cliffs east of Sandy Bay. Our mission is to locate and catch five rather special female sea lions. Each is carrying a set of electronic instruments that were glued to their backs a few months earlier, comprising a satellite transmitter to tell us how far they travel at sea, a time-depth recorder to log their dives, and a VHF radio transmitter to allow us to find them on land. Boots on and windproofs packed, we set out about midday, heading for the far end of Sandy Bay. We pass tail-bobbing pipits on the grassy foreshore, banded dotterels scurrying along the beach, giant petrels that are milling about without an obvious purpose, and a group of about 20 male sea lions enjoying a prolonged siesta on the sand. Some of the sea lions are lying as close as sausages on a barbecue. A few are draping a flipper across the neighbour. Nick says the scientific term for this tactile behaviour is thigmotaxis. I guess it is a sort of sea lion social security.

In these guys, however, we are not the slightest bit interested. To quote the title of one of my daughter's first and most cherished books, we're going on a bear hunt. Sea bears, in this case. As the popular American children's book proceeds to say, we're going on a bear hunt and we're not scared! Well, I know that two of us are not. I have to say I am feeling the weight of my apprehension. My job is to carry, in addition to my cameras and warm clothing (just in case the weather does turn subantarctic), 30 kilograms of anaesthetic and oxygen equipment. Nick made it sound simple. Once we have located the female and netted her, my job is to pop on the anaesthetic mask and, bingo, we have a sea bear subdued and deeply asleep. There are usually four or five people on an expedition of this kind. On this expedition we have two experienced members and one nervously excited volunteer.

Scientists like Nick and Simon are studying these sea lions for more than just curiosity about the way sea lions socialise and breed, how they bring up their young, where they travel and forage, what they eat and how deep they dive. What is driving this research more than anything is concern about the future of the species in the face of accidental drowning of dozens of sea lions each year in the nets of squid trawlers operating on the Auckland Islands Shelf.

For the moment, though, all I can think about is the weight of the gear and how far we might have to walk with it on a bush-clad island four and a half kilometres long and up to two and a half kilometres wide.

Oh, and another thing, sea lions are carnivorous animals, large, bold and boisterous. I imagine they take exception to being messed with.

TWO

LIKE AN ABORIGINAL hunter-gatherer, blowpipe at the ready, Nick edges nearer his quarry, half crouching, his every movement slow, deliberate, noiseless. He lifts the metre-long pipe to his mouth, takes aim, and with cheeks bulging, delivers a short sharp blast of air down the pipe.

'Pooophhh!'

A syringe with a fluffy tail mounted on it darts towards the quarry, bites into golden fur and discharges a clear liquid into the muscular flank of a recumbent female sea lion. The sea lion, full-grown and weighing 130 kilograms, scarcely flinches. She makes no sound. But she does know something strange is happening and, raising herself up on powerful foreflippers, she sniffs the brown pup at her side as if to reassure it, then begins wandering towards the nearby rata forest at a steady rolling gait.

The syringe dart drops to the ground, its job done, and Nick moves in to collect it. He lets the sea lion walk on into the gnarled goblin forest but keeps her in sight. She moves about 20 metres into the shade of the rata from the semi-open shrubland where she was dreamily suckling her pup. On her back are the instruments so precious to the research. We watch and wait. There is time to pack up the radio receiver and aerial that picked up the beeping VHF signal from the transmitter on her back.

After ten minutes the injected sedative, Hynoval, appears to be taking effect. She is a touch groggy. To be sure it is working Nick decides to leave her for another ten minutes. His veterinary training has taught him to be cautious when it comes to sedating and anaesthetising sea lions. He would not risk a knockout dose by injection with the dart syringe. First, there is the problem of estimating the animal's weight and thus the dosage. It would be easy to give a lethal overdose. Second, the sea lion might make a run for the water before the anaesthetic took effect, and in the water she would face certain death by drowning. Safer it is to give the sedative first, net her then administer a gas anaesthetic.

That is why I am now gripping a black suitcase in one hand and oxygen bottle in the other, and why Simon is ready to go into action with one of two custom-made nets. Although roughly the size of a whitebait scoop net, these nets are heavy-duty jobs. The handle is fashioned from heavy alloy and the two poles that extend the mouth of the net are made of strong but flexible fibreglass. The net material itself is a dense fine-mesh nylon that tapers to a head end where the nylon is of double thickness. A hemmed round opening at the end allows the snout of the animal to protrude.

Nick and Simon, carrying a net each, circle round the sea lion. I stand in the wings, white knuckles on the anaesthetic gear. Simon enters within her danger radius and she roars a warning while standing her ground. The pup scampers away, seeking a safer place. He will not go far. Its mother heads in another direction only to find the sky darkening round her. She struggles but her struggling serves only to drive her deeper into the net and finally her head is secure in the tapered end. She is still for a moment. At a word from Nick, Simon dives on her upper body and Nick gets his arms around her foreflippers and mid-body, muttering something about how this seems a lot easier than capturing an unsedated animal. So far, so good. Now for the anaesthetic.

I whip open the case, turn on the gas (Isoflurane, which Nick says is a Rolls Royce anaesthetic used in hospitals – only the best for his animals) and dial up maximum oxygen flow, as previously instructed. An inflatable black bag connected to the gear fills with the mixture. Now for the business end of things. Simon lifts the sea lion's head a fraction and I thrust a heavy rubber mask over her protruding snout. Curiously, the smell of her is more redolent of the earth than of the sea. It is a pleasant animal smell, a bit dog-like. All we can do now is wait. We are waiting for the sea lion to breathe in. Here is an animal that can hold its breath for ten minutes or more. But after the chase on land and the struggle in the net we expect her to breathe within 30 seconds, and she does. She takes two breaths in quick succession then, after a pause, a few more. Within two minutes she is away with the undersea fairies. She is snoring. It is not unlike a full-blown human snore.

Male sea lions are no use in this sort of experiment. They disperse widely after the breeding season. The scientists would almost certainly never see the gear again if it were deployed on males. A female with a pup, on the other hand, will return more or less to the same place to feed its young. The pups in the experiment are fitted with transmitters, too, so that even if the one placed on the mother falls off, the scientists will be able to locate her through her pup.

The recaptured sea lion, breathing comfortably with eyes shut, is oblivious to the next crucial stage. The net is off her and Nick is cutting free the three devices arranged in a line on her back. They were glued to a backing of wetsuit material that was in turn glued to the animal's furry coat. Nick slices between device and the backing material, which will remain harmlessly on the sea lion till she moults next April. Both the VHF and satellite transmitters carry small antennae; the time-depth recorder is a metal cylinder about the size of a small torch and worth over four thousand dollars. It contains a microprocessor that automatically records the time, depth and duration of each dive. Correlated with the satellite data, each dive can be plotted on a map. All instruments deployed like this have to withstand the rough and tumble of sea lion life. They must stand up to being rolled on and squashed between the sea lion and rocks or trees. They also have to withstand the crushing pressure of deep ocean.

Nick examines the wear and tear on the instruments. Some of the protective rubber on the satellite antenna has worn away, exposing the wire underneath. But the epoxyresin casing on the transmitters carries only a few superficial scratches. This sea lion has done her job for science. She will not be bothered again.

The sea lions involved in the research are helping paint a picture of where their kind generally feed and at what depths. Given enough data, the scientists might eventually be able to inform the fishing industry about where sea lions feed in any particular month and warn trawlers to keep clear. It is in the interest of the fishing companies to cooperate. In a boom squid season they stand to lose plenty if too many sea lions are caught early on and fishing is curtailed by government decree.

We pack up the gear and withdraw to look for her pup. He has looped back more or less to where we first found the pair. Weighing about 40 kilograms, he is easily netted, and this time Simon and I hold him tightly within the net while Nick recovers the transmitter. Although only nine months old, he is a muscular ball of energy and it takes a firm grip to keep his foreflippers still. His mother will be asleep for another 20 or 30 minutes yet.

By two o'clock in the afternoon we have bagged the first set of instruments. When Nick dials up the frequency of another female, we get a beeping reply straight away. We catch her not 200 metres from where the first one was caught. There are splashing sounds and pup-like yelps coming from within the forest, and Simon mentions the existence of a small lake, Lake Teal, nearby that is a gathering place for pups – a nursery swimming pool.

Then Nick locks on to a signal from a third female. It is faint but it is a signal. We can hardly believe our luck. Carrying the recapture gear, we plod upwards through the rata forest in pursuit of her. Although we are feeling the effects of two nights at sea, we know that when the subantarctic sun shines on you, you must make the most of it. An hour later a third set of instruments is recovered. Within the electronic wizardry of this female's time-depth recorder, as with the others, is a record of up to 7,000 dives – data never before obtained at this time of year. Summer diving behaviour was studied over the previous two summers. One female reached a depth of 522 metres but this was exceptional. Most dives were to depths less than 200 metres and took four or five minutes. A maximum time of 12.1 minutes was recorded. The research is showing that New Zealand sea lions dive deeper and stay submerged longer than any other sea lion species.

The third female beeping at us has us walking for 20 minutes through the rata. It is mostly open under the canopy – a subantarctic woodland criss-crossed with sea lion tracks. While we wait for the sedative to work on this third animal, we hear another mother and pup approaching. The pair call alternately, a mixture of bleat and bark, and they pass close to us using a well-worn route. So far from the sea, they seem anything other than marine mammals. More like bears. Despite a long evolutionary path, perhaps they still have recall of forest as natural habitat.

It is dim in the forest by the time we complete our work with the third female and her pup. Dusk is coming, although the daylight is only slowly submitting to the night.

Out on the coastal turf again, heading back to the hut, we pass a mob of more than 20 sea lions lying quietly on the bouldery shore. To our amazement, there is a set of instruments on the back of one of them. Although it is getting late Nick decides we ought to try to capture her. He readies the blowpipe syringe and moves gingerly amongst the sea lions. Some animals roar at him but he knows their limits – the boundary between bluff and belligerence. We shepherd the darted female away from the water, which would endanger her in a sedated state if she rushed back into it. She cooperates. There is no sign of her pup. Dusk is well advanced before we have her instruments in the bag.

We stash the heavy anaesthetic gear and nets ready for use next day on the fifth and last animal co-opted for the mid-year experiment, and head on home, well satisfied at having completed four-fifths of five days' work in seven hours. We walk along in silent contemplation of the gathering darkness, watching where we step in case there are sea lions asleep in the big Poa tussocks. In any tactile encounter with sea lions there is a risk you might get bitten. Our medical kit contains five different kinds of antibiotics for such an eventuality. To operate safely in a place like this you need to be well provisioned and careful to avoid fires with cooking and heating equipment. You need to maintain a radio link and, above all, watch your step.

It is dark as we make our way, leaden-footed, along Sandy Bay beach to the hut. The wind has died away, and with it the chill. Nothing much has changed for the sea lions at their beach bachelor pad. They lie above the high tide mark, snoozing into the night, although there are a few newcomers among them. Their coats, still wet, shine in the faint night light. Above the swish of wave on sand, we hear a yellow-eyed penguin greeting its mate.

We have been on a bear hunt for sure, and we will sleep ten hours tonight, although I would not be surprised if the four-metre swells of the previous two days cause the hut to rock a bit.

THREE

IN 1990, IN THE DUNES at the eastern end of Sandy Bay, a visitor to Enderby Island picked up an artefact. It was a fishhook. Given the long seafaring history of the Auckland Islands, the discovery of a fishhook might not seem out of the ordinary. But this one was immediately intriguing. It was made of bone and clearly Maori in origin – a slender, one-piece fishhook, with a small groove carved into the foot of it for tying bait. The same visit turned up another artefact, a chert flake of the kind pre-European Maori used for cutting fibre or meat. Roughly oval, it was shaped to fit firmly into the palm of the hand for use as a knife.

How long had these artefacts been here? Who brought them? No one will ever answer these questions with certainty. What we do know is that the Port Ross area has a unique place in Polynesian history. In the 1840s a group of more than sixty Maori and Moriori arrived at Port Ross from the Chatham Islands to create Polynesia's southernmost settlement. From all angles, it is a bizzare tale. To begin with, the new settlers arrived just two years after an exploring British naval expedition under Captain James Ross called in on its way to Antarctica. Ross was impressed by the harbour. He envisaged a penal settlement here or a whaling base. His scientists included botanist Joseph Hooker, whose name would later be attached to the sea lions. For the future use of castaways, should any ships be wrecked at the Auckland Islands, the expedition put ashore pigs on the main island (augmenting the population started by Bristow) plus some sheep and poultry. On Enderby, Ross left a fancy breed of French rabbits.

The first Maori to reach the Auckland Islands came with sealing ships in the early 1800s. Maungahuka was the southern Maori name for these islands, a reference to a hilly place where albatross down was found. Among the earliest Maori visitors was a North Island Ngati Mutunga chief, Matioro, who later turned up in the Chatham Islands with some of his people. They enslaved Chathams Moriori. In the spring of 1842, Matioro chartered a Sydney-based brig, *Hannah*, to deliver about forty of his people and a smaller contingent of Moriori slaves to the Auckland Islands, 500 kilometres to the south. The reasons for such a desperate move can only be guessed at now. Fear of a French reprisal appears to have been a factor. The Ngati Mutunga chief was implicated in the killing of some Frenchmen on a French whaler in the Chatham Islands some years earlier.

When Maori and Moriori arrived at Port Ross, they were said

to be so appalled by the soil, climate and food resources they wanted to go back immediately. The *Hannah*'s skipper had other ideas. Having been paid 150 pigs for the charter, he figured the deal could come unstuck. Abruptly he weighed anchor, abandoning the settlers. At first they built their huts on a headland on the southern shores of Port Ross but some of the group later established a village on Enderby Island. We can but speculate at the hardship and misery they endured.

For food, they would have relied on, among other things, the pigs released by Bristow and Ross, although from all accounts the pig meat was tough and fishy (in harsh winters, the pigs resorted to eating kelp along the shoreline, and they still do). Other protein sources included ducks, albatrosses, petrels and their eggs, and the seals – mainly fur seals, sea lions and elephant seals – that had survived the slaughter by sealing expeditions. They also tried planting potatoes and other vegetables but found conditions poor for crops.

For seven years they struggled on. Then came a miracle. English whalers arrived at Port Ross in December 1849, determined to establish a prosperous colony despite the remote location. This was about as far as you could get from the mother country. They were led by Charles Enderby, a son of the famous London whaling company, Samuel Enderby and Sons. Bristow had worked for this firm. To attract investment, the company had published a prospectus for a permanent shore whaling base that could also carry out ship repairs, refits and victualling services. Blindly optimistic, its authors portrayed a Garden of Eden. Whatever grew in England would also flourish in the Auckland Islands, they said. An acre of Auckland Islands land could support as many sheep as six acres in Australia.

But there were shocks from the outset, not the least the presence of a Maori settlement. Enderby had written: 'The settlers will be free from aboriginals, there being none on the island.' How deflating it must have been for Enderby to learn of the existence of a Maori settlement. Nonetheless, bearing a commission from Queen Victoria that accorded him the status of Lieutenant-Governor of the Auckland Islands (the islands were not considered to be a part of New Zealand at that time), he is reported to have proclaimed to the assembled Maori and Moriori: 'I am the Lord of the Island.' But he had the sense to swear in as constables Matioro and fellow chief Ngatere, and pay compensation to the Maori for their land and pigs. Thus was born the settlement of Hardwicke, named after the whaling company's principal.

Three ships landed the colonists and their supplies, including 18 prefabricated buildings, at Erebus Cove, a sheltered mainland site on the western shores of Port Ross. Within weeks a small town stood where there had once been dense rata forest. The Lieutenant-Governor had a large house; families had cottages. A barracks was erected for the single men. A store, workshop and chapel were also built.

That first summer was wet and windy. Cold acidic soils stunted the crops. The potatoes were like marbles and turnips grew as small as radishes. By autumn the first of the southern right whales were expected to show up in Port Ross and adjacent coastal waters for the winter breeding season. They failed to appear, though, and when whaling remained poor the next winter, the writing was on the wall for the Hardwicke Settlement. Clearly, the company had underestimated the decimating impact of earlier whaling on shore-based operations. From then on, only deep-water whaling with factory ships would turn a profit. The Hardwicke Settlement had missed the boat.

Its population peaked at about three hundred, including the Chatham Islands people and visiting seamen. As the stress of meagre subsistence farming, a testing climate and the lack of whales mounted, things grew fractious. Shoe Island in the middle of the harbour was declared a prison and unruly members of the population were despatched there or threatened with it.

Enderby Island provided the only light relief. Groups boated over for picnics and recreation on the coastal turf – and a change of air. The killing of an occasional sea lion provided some excitement.

One of the shortest colonial experiments in British history, lasting just two years and nine months, came to an end in August 1852 when a British naval vessel collected the survivors. But not the Maori and Moriori. Some of the Chatham Islanders had wanted to leave there and then but were refused passage. Two years later a number of them were shipped to Stewart Island where a Rakiura chief gave them permission to settle at Port Adventure. In early 1856, the last of the original Auckland Islands colonists were uplifted in a chartered brig. Together with their relatives and slaves from Stewart Island and the Foveaux Strait area, 47 souls all told, they returned to Waitangi in the Chatham Islands, thirteen and a half years after emigrating south.

Ironically, a few weeks before the demise of the whaling settlement, a whale swam into Port Ross. A female in calf, perhaps arriving early for the calving season, it was attacked and killed forthwith. It yielded five tons of whale oil, some of which might have later fuelled the street lamps of London, and an amount of baleen that could have gone on to stiffen the corsets of fashionable ladies of Europe.

FOUR

BREAKSEA GIRL is back – back from Campbell Island and looking for whales. Skipper Lance Shaw radios an invitation to the sea lion team on Enderby to join the vessel for a tour of Port Ross to count the southern right whales still using the harbour after the winter breeding. With our mission accomplished well within the alloted five days, and with five sets of instruments safely to hand and the weather deliciously warm and millpond calm, we feel we can shout ourselves a harbour cruise.

On board, the talk is of encountering five-metre waves and strong winds in the vicinity of Campbell Island. Eyes roll. No doubt stomachs did, too. For the moment, though, *Breaksea Girl* is slipping through water so still we can see the bottom of the harbour at depths of up to ten metres. It is a superb day for whale spotting.

'Whale, port side!' someone shouts, with adrenaline-pumping fervour. At once, our vessel's low rumble is silenced and we drift, turning slowly. At 200 metres we see the whale blow, and a fraction of a second later the sound effects reach us. How the Hardwicke people must have longed to see and hear this.

'Young one, by the look,' says skipper Lance Shaw from the door of the wheelhouse. He has helped count whales here before on scientific expeditions. 'It might just come over.'

It does. When its back breaks the surface with no dorsal fin, it looks like a smooth basalt boulder sliding gently towards us, without a bow wave. Near the vessel, the whale submerges a metre or so and now we can clearly see its head, its improbably curved mouthline set high up on its head, surprisingly small flippers and a scattering of crusty white growths, called callosities, on its upper body. It is about eight metres long, certainly a juvenile.

Breaksea Girl is almost stationary as the whale closes in. It seems to want to touch the vessel. As it moves towards the bow I rush ahead along the deck, hoping for some close-up photographs as it passes. I lean out over the rail. It is a breathtaking moment for both of us, for the whale chooses this moment to blow. Before I know it I am performing a hongi with a whale – in Maori terms, an exchange of breath and thus life force. The whale's 'breath' is a very fine water vapour, which is faintly fishy to my nose. It wafts past me, coating the camera lens. I see the lips of the double blowhole quiver as the animal exhales then sucks in air, including, I suppose, a few molecules of my own exhaled air. We exchange breath but not words. This animal's intelligent communication depends on whistles, squeaks and moans incomprehensible to me. Of what does it speak? Of an undersea society involving extended families, long migrations, playful encounters with sea lions? Is there a memory – and stories handed down – of the killing time when the sea turned red from the harpooning? Apparently not. This whale seems utterly unafraid, at least while the propeller is still. It slips away towards the harbour entrance and we continue our search in the other direction, towards Erebus Cove.

Right whales were so named because they were the 'right' ones to hunt. Slow movers, they were easy to catch from a whaleboat. They tended to float after lancing and rendered generous quantities of oil and baleen relative to the catching effort. Of all the great whales, right whales are considered to be the most approachable. Big ones, round as submarines, grow to 18 metres and 80 tonnes. Their callosities identify them not only as a race but individually. These patches of rough skin are colonised by parasitic worms, whale lice and barnacles, which together add to the prominence of the callosities. Their bristly two-metre curtains of baleen, coveted by the whalers of old, enable them to forage krill, copepods and other planktonic crustaceans. While feeding, a right whale trawls through a shoal of krill with its mouth fully open. As the water flows out the sides, the plankton is left trapped and entangled in the baleen. In this way, a large right whale can sieve two tonnes of krill a day. White sharks and killer whales are enemies of these whales, which defend themselves mainly by lashing out with their huge tail flukes. The main enemy, man, has gone.

Nowadays winter scientific expeditions to the Auckland Islands can see a hundred whales or more in Port Ross.

Off Shoe Island, the Alcatraz of Port Ross, where blond tussocks overhang low cliffs built of vertical columnar rock – the grilles of an old jail – we encounter a right whale cow and calf. We give them a wide berth. Mother is defensive, noticeably putting herself between our vessel and her calf. Another adult appears, head out of water, off Erebus Cove. It shows us its elegant outstretched tail flukes, which are perhaps four metres wide, before sliding from view. The water must be deep at this point to enable it to perform such a dive.

The skipper has a destination in mind – Laurie Harbour, the narrow head of Port Ross, its most sheltered water. Two more whales are ahead of us, as if leading the way but in reality we are probably herding them. They will double back later. By late afternoon we are tucked up at anchor close to the northern side of the harbour, where the rata grows tall and casts reflections well out into the water on this fine day. The weather is changing, however, and the forecast is for strong winds and rain coming out of the north or northeast. Port Ross lies exposed to these conditions.

The storm strikes overnight, bringing with it a dense misty cloud that veils all but the lowest levels of the main island. Even the far side of Laurie Harbour is blurred. The murk is both wet and highly mobile. It is scooting past the bluffs above our anchorage, releasing frequent showers that are connected by periods of drizzle. At last the Auckland Islands are living up to the reputation recorded in the literature over the years – 'abominable climate', 'extraordinarily bleak', 'incessant rain', 'dismal banishment'.

Lance decides to sit tight for the day. He lights a diesel heater in the sleeping area below to ward off the chill damp.

I seize the chance to explore ashore. No bones about it, I want to see Erebus Cove and savour history. Simon, young and fit and not the least bit fazed by the weather, is a starter, too. We are dropped off by dinghy. This is a day for the Swazi Milair breathable nylon raincoat, Seal Skinz socks (dry feet guaranteed), hot thermos, chocolate bars and – and yes, why not? – a cheerful disposition. Having plotted on the wheelhouse chart a cross-country route through the bush to Erebus Cove, a distance of about one and a half kilometres, we set off. We are soon on hands and knees, bush-bashing through thickets of the robust grass tree *Dracophyllum*.

No satellite navigation here; no sun, either, to help direct us. The bush goes on and on. At times I worry about whether we are getting turned inland, off course in the dense sodden bush. We sweat inside our waterproofs. It would be good to see a castaway depot, however run-down.

Suddenly, trees of a kind we have not encountered before materialise through the mist. They are a kind of native tree daisy, *Olearia lyallii*, and I know we are okay. A botanical oddity, these lanky big-leafed trees have become established at Erebus Cove. No one knows for sure how they came to be here. They could have been introduced accidentally or otherwise by sealers or whalers or Maori, or perhaps birds carried the seed from The Snares, a subantarctic group to the north that is covered in these trees.

Erebus Cove is a noisy place today. Northeast winds near gale-force are tearing at the canopy and driving waves into the spongy banks, which have been undercut by earlier storms. A century and a half of bush regeneration has overridden virtually all traces of the whaler settlement. Old bottles, glass fragments, bits of iron, a broken brick or two, cobblestones from paths long gone . . . there is not much to show of a township that had its own school, church and currency. Underfoot, thick dark leaf-mould overtopping peat has been rooted up at intervals by pigs descended from those put ashore by the Bristow and Ross expeditions. Some of the rootings look like they could have been done that day but we neither see nor hear pigs.

What the pigs rip up, the sea lions flatten. We happen upon a female, contentedly feeding her plump nine-month-old pup. Beside them on the forest floor are two pieces of squid, puzzlingly fresh and intact and no doubt regurgitated by the female.

Not far from this wildlife surprise is one of a historical nature – two slipways cut out of the bank above the high-tide mark. The larger slipway is big enough to take a whaleboat, the smaller appears designed as a canoe haul-out. In swotting the history of the Auckland Islands I do not recall any reference to these built features but there they are, a bit overgrown now with roots protruding along the sides, but still serviceable. The larger slipway is neatly cut and squared. The castaway boatshed a little farther along the shoreline of the cove is an obvious relic and well documented. Ramshackle now, it is full of old collapsed wooden crates and broken bottles.

But the most conspicuous links with past settlement here are the flax bushes dotted along the cove's rocky shoreline. A New Zealander might not think twice about them but the fact is that the common flax of mainland New Zealand, harakeke *Phormium tenax*, does not naturally occur here. It was planted, probably by the Maori and Moriori settlers, who came from the Chatham Islands. Told by early sealers and whalers that harakeke was missing from the landscape, they could well have packed some cuttings aboard the brig *Hannah* on the migration voyage and got planting as soon as they arrived. From flax, they could make ropes, garments, baskets, mats, nets and other things. Flax helped these people survive here longer than the English. Adding mystery to the story of the Auckland Islands flax is the assurance that it is not of Chatham Islands origin. It may have come originally from Taranaki, home of the Ngati Mutunga people who invaded the Chathams.

More sobering testimony to the place of Erebus Cove in Auckland Islands history is to be found a short walk through the bush – a small cemetery containing six marked graves. It is surrounded these days by a relatively new picket fence whose sturdiness is designed to deter pigs. The cemetery served not only the failed Hardwicke Settlement but also the shipwreck era that followed soon afterwards. Here lie four shipwrecked mariners and two babies. One of the mariners, John Mahony, second mate of the *Invercauld*, died of starvation after his vessel was wrecked at the Auckland Islands in 1864. The two babies, each about three months old, died in 1850 and 1851. And what of the Maori dead, e nga mate? They were carried back to the Chathams for reburial.

In October 1865, Her Majesty's Colonial Steam-Sloop *Victoria*, an Australian government vessel, visited Erebus Cove and left a message that lives on, if faintly. It was carved into a sawn face of a large rata tree and read:

> H.M.C.S. VICTORIA Norman
> In Search of Shipwrecked People
> Oct 13th 1865

Pruned and painted black and white by the crew, the Victoria Tree would have been a prominent feature on the shoreline at one time. But it is gradually rotting away and only a protective A-frame structure makes it stand out today.

Like the crew of the *Victoria*, Simon and I have a vessel waiting. We pause only long enough to read the message and touch the tree out of reverence for what it symbolises. The day's greyness is unrelieved and the chill presses closer. It is still blowing hard. What would we have done on such a day in the Hardwicke Settlement? Thank goodness for chocolate bars and a thermos.

FIVE

IT IS TIME to say goodbye to Enderby and the Auckland Islands. A lot of people have come and gone over the years. Some were mighty glad to see the back of the place. Between 1864 and 1907, at least eight ships were wrecked at the Auckland Islands, with the loss of 121 lives. In those times the Auckland Islands lay in the path of ships using the wind-assisted Great Circle Trading Route from Australia to Europe via Cape Horn. Once you had cleared the New Zealand subantarctic islands it was plain sailing all the way to South America.

Early in the era, however, the Auckland Islands were wrongly charted. The charts put the group about 45 kilometres to the south of where they actually were. In other words, vessels aiming to pass to the north of the islands were at grave risk. The first ship to come unstuck in this way was the Valparaiso-bound *Invercauld* in May 1864. Caught in a storm, she shattered herself on a reef below towering cliffs at the north-west point of the main island. Nineteen of the 25-strong crew managed to gain the shore and scale the cliffs but only three survived in the end. They built a seal skin boat using supple *Dracophyllum* branches for framework and used it to explore the Port Ross Islands. They lived off albatrosses, shags, shellfish and giant herbs such as *Stilbocarpa*, the Macquarie Island cabbage. On Enderby Island they hunted rabbits. After a year they were saved by a Spanish brig that put into Port Ross in the misplaced hope of being able to undertake repairs at the Hardwicke Settlement.

The costliest wreck of all was that of the *General Grant*, a big American-built three-masted barque. On a voyage from Melbourne to London in 1866 with a cargo of wool, hides, timber and gold bullion, she foundered on the main island's awesome western coast. Sixty-eight of the 83 passengers and crew perished in the sea or were dashed on the rocks. Five of the 15 survivors died subsequently. By the time they were rescued by a sealing vessel, the ten surviving castaways of the *General Grant* had been marooned for 18 months.

Their experience prompted New Zealand authorities to step up provisioning for castaways at the Auckland Islands. Robust depots were erected, the first at Enderby Island, just above Sandy Bay. The depots were equipped with tools, matches, fishing gear, clothing, blankets, medicine, utensils and food in the form of tinned meat and biscuits. The truly courageous – or desperate – had recourse to a compass and sailing instructions for reaching New Zealand. Looters were warned with messages such as this: 'The curse of the widow and fatherless light upon the man who breaks open this box, whilst he has a ship at his back.'

Perhaps the unluckiest castaways of all were those of the *Derry Castle*. On the night of 21 March 1887, a wet and squally night, the iron barque was dashed to pieces on the northern point of Enderby Island, the northernmost land in the whole group. Had she been on a course a hundred metres to the north, the *Derry Castle* would have been in clear water with South America the next landfall. Bound for England out of Geelong, the *Derry Castle* sank with her cargo of Australian wheat on a reef that now bears her name. Of the 23 souls on board, only seven crew members and the one passenger survived the angry sea and battering rocks. Most were barefoot and thinly clad. For days afterwards the survivors, including the passenger, James McGhie, kept picking up bodies on the shore and burying them by digging into the cold soil with a knife. They also collected any wheat washed up and ate it raw.

The castaway depot at Sandy Bay should have been a godsend. Instead, having been raided in earlier years, it contained only a bottle of salt. The little A-frame depot was too small to accommodate them all so they built circular huts thatched with reeds and tussock grasses. For the first few days the survivors ate everything raw – seabirds, seals and shellfish.

When McGhie found a revolver cartridge, fortunes changed. The gunpowder became a fire lighter. In the second month someone found an axehead, perhaps left behind by sealers. It was put to use in the construction of a punt about three metres long by one metre wide. Shipwreck timber contributed to the framework, nails were recycled and strips of iron sheeting became caulking.

With the punt, the *Derry Castle* survivors aimed to reach the castaway depot at Erebus Cove, a tantalising white beacon in the distance. Two of the seamen paddled the punt across to Erebus Cove where they found the treasure they hoped for – tinned food, matches, candles, a rifle and ammunition, and clothing. They could dress up. The clothes included government-issue three-piece suits with a distinctive yellow stripe. To deter sealers and others from stealing the suits, the New Zealand Government had ordered the yellow stripe woven into the material. And there was a rowboat. And proper shelter.

But the windfall was not without a sour note. McGhie would later allege that the pair in the punt, anticipating a long wait for a rescue vessel, cached food for themselves before returning to pick up the rest of the party on Enderby. In the event, none of the survivors starved. After four months they were rescued by a sealing vessel.

I remember that punt. It was lying, a little worse for wear and weather, on a beach on the main island not far from Erebus Cove when the New Zealand frigate *Southland* called in 1990, carrying a party of conservation and historic heritage people, myself among them. Boxed up for support, the punt was about to make its last and longest trip – to the Southland Museum to become a star attraction in a new subantarctic gallery. Without this mothball treatment, it was bound to disintegrate. It is not easy to preserve artefacts in situ. Besides climatic factors, looters are as active today as they were in the square-rigged days. Relics have slowly disappeared from the Hardwicke Settlement, from the more accessible shipwreck sites, and from huts and lookouts used by coastwatchers in World War II.

On the evening after our prowl around Erebus Cove, and with the wind easing, *Breaksea Girl* puts the sea lion gang ashore at Sandy Bay so we can collect our gear and secure the hut. We shall be on our way home next morning, weather permitting. I feel I know Enderby pretty well. Thanks to the cooperative sea lions I had time to walk across most of the island in those first few days. Unlike the castaways, I was well fed, well togged up and glad to have warm, dry lodgings to go back to at Sandy Bay. I tramped the island's hummocky tundra, which at this time of year is dotted with impossibly large royal albatross chicks. I wandered idly through the rata forest, a setting not unlike the woods in Walt Disney's *Bambi* film, and I saw how the giant herbs of the Enderby Island are recovering now the shorthorn cattle of turn-of-the-century farming activities have been removed. At the forlorn gale-battered *Derry Castle* memorial overlooking the northern reef I stood in respectful and wondering silence.

But perhaps the most enduring image came one sunny afternoon. I spent half an hour observing a female sea lion resting among rocks on top of the island's black undercut western cliffs. She must have walked for an hour or two to get there. But why come to this spot, a field of boulders wholly clad in white lichen and 30 metres above the surging sea? And with not another sea lion as far as the eye could see? As she nosed the air to try to catch a whiff of me, she looked for all the world like a polar bear. I left her to slumber on.

Close by, right at the edge of the cliff, I came upon another object common to this island but, again, somewhat out of place. It was a whip of bull kelp, complete with holdfast. Too heavy for any bird to lift, this piece of kelp must have been deposited here by a wave. But just how high was the wave that hurled it? Ten metres? More? Even allowing for the splash effect of a big swell against a sheer cliff and for water-shredding winds reaching storm force, it must have been quite a wave to strand seaweed this high.

We will soon be heading into the ocean that spawned those sorts of seas. I have one last thing to do on Enderby. From the huts, I run up the track and boardwalk to the castaway depot for a photograph. The depot is a weatherboard A-frame about head-high at the apex. At one time it would have been out in the open; now it is enclosed by low forest. An inscription says it was built in 1880. In modern times, it has acquired a protective tanalised timber fence, sturdy enough to resist either a cattle beast rubbing against it, or a pushy sea lion. The lowering afternoon light, softened by a light cloud cover, is just right to show off the parched sand-coloured timbers.

On the way back through a patch of forest to join Nick and Simon – our gear is stacked up ready on the beach to be transferred to *Breaksea Girl* – I am suddenly aware that someone or something is watching me from within the forest. If you feel that sort of energy in the air, you have to stop. I stop and cast an eye around the gnarled rata. Then I see it. A falcon, of the Auckland Islands race of New Zealand falcon. It is perched above head level and only four metres from me. It seems unperturbed by my presence.

As it fluffs its dappled body feathers I notice its legs are turning from the juvenile grey-green to adult yellow. It is probably almost a year old. I knew there was a small population of falcons resident in the Auckland Islands but had not encountered one before.

With soft voice, I say: 'I've got a mate back in Otago who knows quite a lot about you guys. He's called the Lark. Flies with falcons, he does. I'll be sure to tell him I met you.'

The falcon turns its head now, as if reacting to a movement in the bush. It flattens its body and leans forward in launch mode.

A parakeet flashes across the track just then and the falcon, a much larger bird, gives chase. It is surprisingly agile in the air in the confines of the forest. In a few moments I lose sight of it.

Nick and Simon are organising the rubber dinghy for our departure. Sandy Bay is no millpond this time. Stirred up by the northeaster, low brown waves are charging vigorously at the beach. There is another factor – the onset of high tide.

'Stand by to get wet,' warns Nick.

Because of the surf we have no choice but to load the gear into the Zodiac from the channel in the reef – the arrival procedure in reverse. We push Nick out in the orange dinghy, which bucks the waves as he guns the outboard motor. We start wading across the rock platform to the channel with our packs and other gear. The sea is surging across the reef, grey clouds have returned and rain is threatening. The sea is cold to wade through, and it surges to 'oops' level, approaching the waist. Simon and I have to carry the gear on our shoulders or overhead and hope not to be bowled over by a surge. For the first time on the trip I get a sense of the adversity faced by people who have gone before us here.

The next lot at Enderby will be a summer expedition. They will observe the breeding season and count the pups. They will apply a clever formula to arrive at a figure for the season's pup production at Sandy Bay. For now, though, only a handful of sea lions are hauled out. The storm-enhanced high tide has disturbed quite a few young males from their slumbers and prompted them to head to sea again.

Breaksea Girl returns to Laurie Harbour for the night, out of the northeaster's way. Lance, the skipper, spends more time than usual on the radio-telephone, located aft in his cabin. He is trying to work out the weather pattern for the next 36 hours. In this problematic exercise he is assisted by a professional weather-watcher at Invercargill, a former fisherman named Murray Patterson whose advice Lance values beyond words. Lance's livelihood and the lives of his passengers and crew could depend on predictions of bad weather. Murray dishes out information on request to southern ocean mariners like Lance Shaw. On the way down here, I was astonished by Murray's ability to pinpoint critical wind shifts 12 to 20 hours ahead. There are several calls to Murray that night from *Breaksea Girl*. Between them, Lance paces the wheelhouse, studious and tense.

'Not looking great for tomorrow,' he says. 'Forty knots southwest coming away later in the day. Down here forty can get to fifty then sixty knots and before you know it, you're staring down the barrel of storm-force.'

But daybreak sees the northeast gone and cloud swirling round the tops. Lance makes another call to Murray. By nine o'clock, we have a decision.

'We've got a twelve-hour window with moderate southwest. Then she's supposed to come away strong from the northwest – bad news going home,' Lance says curtly. He strokes his greying beard, lights a cigarette, a roll-your-own, and parks himself at the open wheelhouse door, half in the cabin, half out, feet straddling the lip that at sea keeps any water sloshing along the deck from entering the cabin. It is a favourite 'posi' of his, one he uses often while the vessel is under way. Here he can brace himself against the doorframe to counteract the motion. He can see ahead, astern and more of the sky than is visible from the wheelhouse. And he can let the cigarette smoke drift outside.

From the wheelhouse door Lance studies the cloud movement above Port Ross. 'We'll have a go,' he says. 'Poke our nose out anyway.'

By late morning we are rounding the eastern shores of Enderby Island and straightening north. *Breaksea Girl* bucks in a confused sea. The wind is round to the southwest all right, and steady. I tucked into a Paihia Bomb or two after breakfast and feel not the slightest bit seasick. Nonetheless, I prefer to be on deck testing my sealegs for as long as possible at the start of a voyage.

For a while the wind is more or less astern and the passengers can relax on the foredeck, bathing in sunshine for the first time in two days. As our course shifts left to just west of north the foredeck gets wet and we move inside. There is adrenaline in the air, the thrill that comes of not quite knowing what to expect. We are trying to use Murray's 'twelve-hour window' to track as far out to the northwest as possible – insurance against the arrival of headwinds from that direction. If the winds do shift that way, we can bear to the right to take them on the beam and make for shelter at The Snares, which lie between the Auckland Islands and Stewart Island. Lance wants to go there anyway. He envisages our breakfasting at The Snares tomorrow. Then, with time up our sleeve, we will push on to Port Pegasus in southern Stewart Island late in the day and moor overnight there before the last leg to Bluff.

Lance looks slightly less worried now we have the autopilot humming its duo-tone and the Auckland Islands a hazy lump behind us. It might look like another day at the office for him but he would be the first to admit that this office never looks the same two days running. Sea, sky and season interact to make just about every moment unique in terms of the state of the seaway, cloud patterns and lighting. That is especially the case in these latitudes.

Over the next 24 hours we will slip across an oceanic abyss – a cross-section of the Southern Ocean. Ten times the size of the United States, the Southern Ocean freewheels westwards virtually unimpeded by landmasses, with the white continent of Antarctica acting as the hub. In the vicinity of 50 degrees south latitude, where the Auckland Islands lie, ocean occupies over ninety-five percent of the surface of the planet. On a clear day you can see the curvature of the earth. Ocean rules the Blue Planet. Although the surface may appear monotonous and featureless, significant boundaries do exist here. Vast water bodies, defined by temperature and salinity differences, jostle for position both vertically and in the horizontal plane. In this region the water bodies include Subantarctic Surface Water, Antarctic Bottom Water and the low-salinity Antarctic Intermediate Water. Where they meet at the surface, they are called convergences or fronts, and we will cross one of them, the Subtropical Convergence, between The Snares and Stewart Island. Away to the south is the other oceanic front that encircles the Southern Ocean in a wavy line, the Antarctic Convergence. The fronts are generators of marine life on a global scale – tuckshops for everything from phytoplanktons to whales.

Beneath us as we head north is the Auckland Islands Shelf, part of the submerged landmass known as the Campbell Plateau. It is the platform for most of New Zealand's subantarctic islands. Around and within it are upwellings that bring nutrients from abysmal depths. Conspicuous productivity is the result and every subantarctic island advertises it. See, smell and hear it at the Auckland Islands in the form of the seabird colonies, the whales that come to calve in sheltered waters, the sea lions lounging on the sandy shores. These things are the outpourings of a rich cocktail, the bubble and froth.

Nineteenth-century European whalers, sealers and birders laid waste to much of this productivity, and they did so without remorse. They had a job to do. If they felt anything, it was probably that the sea, like a mother, should always be able to provide. The attitude remains widespread. Greed aside, how else do you explain the excesses of driftnetting, the ongoing attempts at whaling in the name of science, and the high-tech plunder of species such as Patagonian toothfish and bluefin tuna in the Southern Ocean?

But people who make a living at sea can experience a sea-change in their thinking. Lance Shaw, in his early fifties, is an example. He used to catch crayfish in Fiordland commercially. But he tired of the daily killing, of ripping tails off crays and throwing the bodies back. He turned to a less exploitive life, first as the skipper of the Fiordland National Park vessel *Renown*. In more recent times, in partnership with his wife Ruth, Lance embarked into nature tourism in southern New Zealand waters, with an occasional bit of charter work thrown in. Lance is a cross between Crocodile Dundee and Barry Crump's Good Keen Man, an adventurous practical man, a diver, photographer and no-holds-barred debater. He did a stint in Vietnam during the war but not as a soldier. He went to check out the politics for himself and confirmed on the spot how screwed up it all was. When it comes to nature conservation, he reckons we are still a long way from a sea-change in public attitudes. We humans are not doing enough despite having all the intelligence in the world.

I feel I ought to be engaging Lance in a deep and meaningful discussion about the sea and all it means to him. But how do you start such a discussion? I leave it. *Breaksea Girl* has settled into a tolerable motion, reaching across the four-metre swells. Lance is at his station by the door, fag in hand, looking seaward with the thoughtful, steady gaze of a farmer. Between the foaming wave-tops, the troughs furrow the ocean surface. He is a ploughman.

Here I am applying a landlubber concept to seafaring. But perhaps we have no choice. Perhaps our understanding of the sea and its ecology is almost as limited as a whale's understanding of what it means to experience the Lark's sort of country – inland ranges, the high country. Where the sea is concerned, we grow up with images that are serpent-haunted. Deep ocean is darkly mysterious and scary. Disorientating, too, hence the expression 'all at sea'. From time to time, we are told there is nowhere left on the planet worth exploring. People have trodden the lot, even the moon. Do not believe it. There are trenches in the ocean floor east of our subantarctic zone that appear unplumbed, over six thousand metres deep. The Southern Alps would be swallowed up without trace in some of these trenches. Instead of booking for a trip to Mars at the end of the 21st century, how about a Jules Verne kind of voyage to inner space, serpents and all?

I could go a game of cribbage right now. You can find reward in looking seaward only for so long. Albatrosses, cape pigeons, petrels and shearwaters fly by us from time to time but in no great concentration. While most of the passengers took to their bunks for long periods on the trip south, I played crib at the dining table in the main cabin with one of the Campbell Island albatross expedition members, Matt Charteris. We crib-pegged our way across the Subtropical Convergence and the seas on either side of it, pausing between deals to observe changes in wave pattern and the squiggle of our track on the screen nearby. But with Matt still on Campbell Island I have lost my cribbage partner.

I lie down with a book. My bunk is in the forepeak where the sides of the vessel curve to meet the bow. Here you can most keenly feel the vessel's pitching, and the mattress lifts and sinks as if it is alive and breathing deeply. Ever present is the sound of water swishing and gurgling depending on the angle and size of the waves. Once you have realised the water is going to stay on the outside of the hull, there is an innately satisfying feeling about snuggling into such a bunk – as if the hull were a membrane separating you from the waters of the womb and the sea your real mother after all, the mother of all life on earth.

Still, we are advised by Lance to belt ourselves into the bunk in case the sea mother does something violent. This is as close as I will get to wearing the sea. And it raises the question of whether the ocean ought to be seen as a barrier between landmasses or rather a saline solution bonding them, a thin sort of glue.

I fall asleep, thinking about the marvels of modern navigation, of how a satellite or series of satellites is keeping watch over us, guiding us every step of the way. We can plot our position at any moment to within one-hundredth of a nautical mile. Every few seconds there is a read-out of distance to go to the next way-point and time to go, the latter an estimate based on current speed. Should someone fall overboard, whoever is on watch will instantly press an 'event' button on the autopilot to pinpoint the location. It takes quite a bit of skill to turn a vessel 180 degrees in a moderate sea and return to pick up the person in the water. The 'event' button, a curiously unemotional term given that it has a vital role in an emergency, provides the necessary precision – the course and distance to get back to the incident.

Hunger more than a change in the vessel's motion wakes me. I get up for dinner and stay on chatting with the crew while watching the evening steal across the eastern horizon. We will remain on the present course till the early morning, unless a major wind shift rules otherwise, then bear east for The Snares: muttonbird city.

SIX

IN NOVEMBER 1791, the Royal Navy ship *Discovery*, under the command of George Vancouver, sailed through these waters bound for the Pacific coast of North America. In daylight and with reasonable visibility they came upon what Vancouver described as 'a cluster of seven craggy islands'. This group of scattered low-lying islands he named The Snares in recognition of their potential hazard to vessels plying the Roaring Forties. Today's mariners, even with tools like GPS and radar, remain just as wary of The Snares because of the lack of a secure anchorage here. The nearest thing to a harbour is Hoho Bay on the main island's east coast where some rocks form a partial breakwater across the mouth of a cove. Vessels over 30 metres in length have a job manoeuvring once inside. There is a stout line attached to the land that they can hook on to but the Department of Conservation is planning to remove it in case the island is invaded by rats or mice. It would take only one pregnant rat or mouse to escape across the mooring line for disaster to strike The Snares.

This group of islands is one of the subantarctic zone's least modified nature reserves. It is the only forested set of islands in the whole Southern Ocean without introduced mammals of any kind. No one is allowed to land without a permit. Most vessels, whether fishing, on tour or on charter, pause only for a short time then move on. Visitors from October to April will observe a wildlife phenomenon – the daily commuting to and from feeding grounds of sooty shearwaters or titi. There are said to be 2.75 million pairs of these muttonbirds breeding at The Snares. That is a colossal number considering the size of these islands, whose land area (341 hectares) amounts to less than half that of Enderby Island. They have burrowed practically every square metre of peat, much of it overtopped by tree daisies of the kind found now at Erebus Cove.

At the height of the breeding season the titi darken the skies around dawn and dusk. Their return from sea is an undignified scramble as birds crash and tumble through the canopy to reach their nests. Sooty shearwaters spend winter in the North Pacific and come south for the summer. The Snares seem to be the choicest titi real estate as these islands support the largest population.

Climate, soil conditions and proximity to feeding grounds are presumably critical factors.

Being just a hundred kilometres south of Stewart Island, The Snares are washed by a relatively warm current emanating from Tasman Sea – the East Australian Current. This produces an annual mean temperature three degrees Celsius warmer than that of the Auckland Islands. The Snares are also linked geologically to Stewart Island. They present chips off an old block of granite from which Stewart Island and Fiordland are formed.

By the time I rise, just after dawn, we are moving into the lee of the main island, North East Island, and cruising along an impressive line of granite cliffs on its eastern side. The sky is alive with sooty shearwaters energetically darting and swooping as if performing stretching exercises before heading seaward for the day. And it is definitely warmer. Protected from the westerly winds and bathed in a pastel sunlight, Hoho Bay, named after a fishing boat, appears an idyllic spot for breakfast. Lance is not so sure. The stern line attached to the shore looks secure but he has his doubts about the mooring for the bow. It appears to be dragging its anchor, and there is a worrying degree of surge inside the natural harbour. Breakfast becomes a rushed affair as a result and we pull out of Hoho Bay.

Next door is an arm of sea just wide enough to admit a dinghy. It is the main landing place for The Snares, and the only safe one. As *Breaksea Girl* noses close to the granite slabs at the entrance to the landing spot, a few fur seal bulls on the rocks stir and begin sparring. Below them in the water, two seal lions, males by the look of their dark fur, are cavorting in a fringe of bull kelp and froth. They twist and arch under water, surfacing every few moments with loud expulsions of air reflecting their exertion. Life is a frolic.

The blades of bull kelp here are an odd colour, displaying gold, amber and yellow hues. No one really knows why. The Auckland

Islands bull kelp is mostly dark brown, as it is on mainland New Zealand. One theory suggests that the kelp is paler at The Snares because it is more exposed to the bleaching effects of sunlight, perhaps by attaching to rocks higher in the tidal range.

On the land, the tree daisies, tussock grasses, ferns and megaherbs appear to form a dense cover but I know from a brief visit in 1990 that under the forest at least there is a lot of open ground, and it is kept open by the trampling impact of millions of webbed feet. After the shearwaters, mottled petrels and common diving petrels, Snares crested penguins are the most numerous birds. There are about 20,000 penguins. They breed only here. Their yellow crest feathers, when dry, give them a punkish appearance. They gather in large groups on steep slippery guano-covered rock faces near the water, looking less than happy with their lot.

At least they have room to move at sea. Pity the land birds on such small oceanic islands. Yet there are plenty of them at The Snares, including three endemic birds – a tomtit, fernbird and snipe. Occasionally species new to the group are blown in from Stewart Island or the mainland. South Island fantails arrived here in the late 1970s or early 1980s and given time in this sort of isolation they, too, might produce a unique race.

People have also known isolation here. In the early 1800s four sealers set something of a castaway record for the subantarctic. They were put ashore at The Snares against their will. Escaped convicts from the Norfolk Island penal settlement, they had been taken on by the English sealing vessel *Adventure* for an expedition into the subantarctic. By the time they reached The Snares, however, the ship was desperately short of food. The captain offered the four Hobson's choice: stay with the ship and starve or try their luck ashore. They chose the island and were given a few potatoes from which to grow crops. During their seven years at The Snares (would Norfolk Island have seemed appealing by comparison?), one of the quartet went mad and was killed by his fellow castaways. He was pushed off a cliff. In 1817 the three survivors were rescued but not tried for the death of their companion. They were deemed to have suffered enough.

There is no adversity in our visit to The Snares, nor any discomfort on the leg to Stewart Island through much of the day. The wind and seas are abaft the beam, the sun is out, temperatures are rising and there is a homecoming mood on board *Breaksea Girl*. We could be rolling down to Rio.

In fact, we roll down to Rakiura, the land of glowing skies. The Maori name for Stewart Island is derived from a traditional love story and the blushing of the suitor in the story when he was denied the hand in marriage of both daughters of a local chief. The island is famous for its sunsets but it is also far enough south to experience the southern aurora, which may also produce a blushing sky.

Lance indulges the sea lion enthusiasts on board by pulling into Ernest Island, a known sea lion haul-out site near the southern entrance to Port Pegasus. Sure enough, there are sea lions lounging at one end of the beach below the island's muttonbirder camp, which is occupied in autumn during the harvest of the sooty shearwater chicks. We drop anchor in the sheltered bay and go ashore by motorised dinghy for a look at the sea lions – a gang of adolescent males, probably between two and six years of age. As we near the empty end of the beach they rise up on their haunches and stampede into the water. I am not used to this precipitate behaviour, which is clearly a response to our presence. No doubt they have been disturbed in the past, perhaps forcibly. In the water, though, they are much less timid. They swim in circles around the boat, pop their heads out within arm's reach and follow along behind like playful puppies.

The island is well wooded with rata, fuchsia, broadleaf and

muttonbird shrub. Crown fern dominates the ground cover. Growing within the fern are clumps of *Stilbocarpa robusta*, the megaherb known to Maori as punui, whose crinkly leaves somewhat resemble rhubarb. A botanical link with the subantarctic, the *Stilbocarpa* has disappeared from the main island through browsing by deer. Old-time Maori muttonbirders would use the hollow flower stems of punui to blow air into split blades of bull kelp, thus forming storage bags or poha for the harvested chicks.

But as far as we are concerned the main act on the island is the sea lions, and as they are in the water and beyond reach we return to *Breaksea Girl*. By now it is early evening. For our last night on board we enter Port Pegasus and anchor in Fright Cove near the southern end of Port Pegasus, an extraordinarily beautiful and non-frightening refuge for vessels our size. Tomorrow, Bluff.

An expedition generates its own momentum, mood and magical moments. Each one is unique. You can never exactly retrace the steps. On an expedition of this kind you set the framework and leave fate, chance, luck and calculated risk to add the flesh and colour. Lance's aim was to get to the Auckland Islands, Campbell Island and back again in 11 days. He is going to do it. He will even have time to put into Halfmoon Bay tomorrow for a feed of fish and chips en route to Bluff.

No less satisfied with their work are the sea lion chaps. We have a bag full of scientific treasure – electronic equipment stripped off the backs of five anaesthetised sea bears. In a few days, back in Wellington, Nick Gales will download a swag of information about the thousands of dives those five females made over the past couple of months and correlate that data with their tracks at sea. For the first time, he will analyse the springtime dive patterns of female Hooker's sea lions. Theirs are journeys to humble our brief skim across the surface of the ocean.

PART IV

Going North

> It keeps eternal whisperings around
> Desolate shores, and with its mighty swell
> Gluts twice ten thousand caverns
>
> JOHN KEATS
> 'The Sea', circa 1820

ONE

IN SPRING, the sea bear goes whaling. By this time most of the right whales have left Port Ross after the winter breeding season but a few still linger in the sheltered waters, some mothers with calves, and one or two adolescents aged five to ten years. The adolescents are curious and outgoing. They often cruise past Enderby Island and probe seawards in search of a meal of krill. At times, the sea bear encounters them off Enderby. She can tell that whales are in the vicinity by their underwater calls, and occasionally she chooses to interact with them, one young male in particular, recognisable by the way the white callosities coat one side of his head. The sea bear seems to know the whales are more relaxed now that calving and mating is over. Besides, her own life is freer. With her pup less demanding of her milk now that he is learning to fish for himself, the sea bear can be distracted by something as irresistibly imposing as a whale.

The young male right whale is special. A six-year-old, not yet breeding, he has come to tolerate the close approach of the sea lions. Moving very slowly forward or wallowing, he allows the sea lions to brush him with their flippers as they sprint past or perform flips above and below his big round body. He swims with his enormous mouth closed. Near where his wavy mouth line begins, a large black eye carefully surveys the sea lions. He has his limits. The sea bear tried one day to lie on the arch of his lower back and for a few moments he entertained the joyrider before deciding to warn her off with a swish of his notched tail, which is wider than the sea lions are long. The sea bear felt his shiny skin beneath her, taut, hard and as dark as the ocean floor 500 metres down. When the young whale, perhaps out of a competitive sense or with delusions of his own agility, breaks into a sprint and works up a speed of ten kilometres an hour – full stretch – he creates a bow wave. The sea lions like that. They get to ride the wave. If he sounds, they dive with him but soon lose interest.

Through winter and into spring the sea bear extends her pup's experience of foraging grounds. Before he gets his first taste of the open sea, she leads him on his longest swim yet – to the inner reaches of Port Ross. They scramble ashore one evening at Erebus Cove, and spend the night camped on the soft peat under big-leaved trees the pup has not seen before. The next day mother and pup move back towards Enderby, passing a small group of right whales whose whistles and clicks fill the underwater world. But they make no contact with the whales. The sea bear has other ideas. She senses it is time to introduce her pup to the open sea. Instead of landing back at their usual spot on the south side of the Enderby, she porpoises on past the island, with her pup doing his best to keep up.

The wind, a keen south-wester, is behind them and creating a lumpy sea as it conflicts with a north swell, the product of a recent storm. To be thrust into such a chop startles the pup at first. He bobs in the waves, bawling his concern when he loses sight of his mother. She surfaces with a snort and calls in turn. She wants him to dive with her. Till now, in waters close to Enderby, he has not been required to dive for more than a minute. He still has his milk teeth, which are soon to be replaced by permanent teeth. Close to shore he has pursued and devoured small fish such as blennies, juvenile cod and pipefish, and he has tangled with giant spider crabs on the sea floor. He discovered that these camouflaged crabs, with bodies wider than his head, were more entertaining than nourishing. Although he saw adult sea lions, including his mother, attack and dismember them in a practised way, he found the crabs awkward to get his mouth around. If he were not careful their legs would wrap around his head and their claws would prick him. Octopuses, on the other hand, were softer and delicious eating, but he had yet to learn properly how to prise them from their underwater holes. He had found, through trial and error, that the shellfish near his landing place were generally too difficult to eat – shellfish such as the white-footed paua and blue mussels on the wave-washed rocks and small southern clams couched on the sandy floor of the harbour.

Now, clear of the harbour and land and with her pup nearby, the sea bear treads water. She has seen a disturbance on the surface caused not by the wind but by fish. She has seen the ripples produced by schooling jack mackerel, which flash their silver bellies, quick as reef fish. Although adult mackerel are more commonly found in deeper water, these younger ones sometimes school inshore near the surface. They are fast and wary. The sea bear catches the pup's attention in the choppy seaway. Then, curling her pliable body and becoming for an instant a pale-brown semi-circle above the surface, she dives. To reduce her buoyancy, she exhales before diving. Her nostrils pinch together to shut out the water and she disappears below in a trail of small bubbles. Her pup follows, impressed by the darkness below, a sign of depth. The bubbles, from air trapped in the sea bear's fur, begin to thin out as she stops descending and starts to round on the mackerel, now above mother and pup. The mackerel do not yet know they are being stalked. Against this kind of predator their lateral armour plating – thin lines of hardened scales down each side, just below the blue-green shading of their backs – will offer little protection.

From 20 metres away the sea bear makes her angled upwards lunge towards the silver bellies. Neck extended and stroking the water powerfully with her foreflippers, she quickly reaches attack speed, about 30 kilometres an hour. Over the last few metres she folds her foreflippers tightly against her side and, with clamped hindflippers providing steerage, she becomes a torpedo. She times her attack superbly well, seizing one of the larger fish in the school just under the surface. It lies crossways in her mouth as her momentum shoots her clear of the water. For a second or two she is airborne. Before the pup can catch up with her the other mackerel have streaked well away from the terror and the sea bear is shredding her catch, parts of which the pup snaffles eagerly. More to the point, though, he has learnt something about foraging in open water. In the course of his training his mother will demonstrate that fish smaller than this can be swallowed whole but larger fish are processed at the surface, where the boniest parts are discarded.

The sea bear, on dives to the ocean floor, has encountered jack mackerel many times in mid-water situations or near the bottom – and more often than not she has been left snapping at empty water. During foraging trips she will try to seize any fish off its guard but cannot rely for sustenance on any one species. This is not the case with octopus. They are a staple item. So are arrow squid. Both are easier to pick off than mackerel.

After a couple of minutes at the surface she descends again, with her pup shadowing her. Here the water is about 80 metres deep, well short of her normal range. But it will be new territory for her pup, which till now has led mostly a landlubber existence. Thirty million years of seafaring ancestry have prepared him for this moment.

TWO

BUBBLES STREAM OFF mother and pup as they descend at a steep angle through the first ten metres. Their flattened fur is dense enough to keep the skin dry no matter how long or deep they dive. At 25 metres, farther than the pup has gone before, the sea bear pauses to check on his progress. She doubles around him and gives him an encouraging prod. She murmurs approval, a soft whinny. The light is dimmer at this depth but he can still see well.

Like marine mammals the world over, his eyes are designed for underwater vision. He sees better in water than in air. In water, the large rounded fish-eye lens refracts the light precisely to achieve a clear focus. On land his vision is adequate but he is a trifle nearsighted. Only in bright sunlight, when the pupil contracts to a narrow slit, does the focus approach underwater sharpness. A sea lion's vision deep down in the ocean is challenged by declining light levels and a relentless pressure that increases with depth. To cope with low-light conditions, the retina of the eye is backed by a layer of guanine crystals that gather light and reflect it back through the retina. This enhances the retina's function in gloomy or near-dark conditions. It also makes the eyes appear to glow in the dark. Underwater, sea lion eyes bulge, and a clown-like surrounding white ring accentuates the bulge. To protect the eyes from water pressure, the outer layers contain a tough fibrous protein called keratin.

Unaware of these marvels of adaptation, the pup plunges onwards. His world is reducing to a dim blue-green expanse. And still there is no substance to it, nothing he can relate to in the way of rocks or sand or anything that resembles food. He feels for the first time the impact of pressure but pays it no more attention than might a child cuddled by a blanket. Inside him, though, things are changing.

From the time his nostrils shut like valves as he began the dive, his heartbeat slowed down. It reduced from 80 beats or more a minute to about a quarter the rate. Now his blood is circulating more slowly and conservatively but he has plenty of it, as has his mother. They have almost twice as much blood as land mammals of similar size. This means they have more oxygen in circulation. Critical, too, is the presence of generous quantities of the compound myoglobin, which, like haemoglobin in humans, acts as an oxygen transporter. In sea lions, the myoglobin saturates muscle tissue, turning it richly red, almost black. It sustains oxygen supply to the muscles. It keeps up their strength even after increasing water pressure has forced a radical rerouting of the blood away from the muscles and extremities and into the vital organs, especially the brain.

Near the sea floor, 80 metres down, the sea bear comes upon a giant Cyanea jellyfish, exquisitely decorated in shades of red and brown, its vibrating frilled body about the size of her head and tentacles trailing over almost two metres. In the faint light she can see the pup still descending and waits for him to catch up. By ignoring the jellyfish she demonstrates it is not something he should tangle with. Its stinging cells can cause pain to a sea lion.

The rocky bottom of the ocean is now in visual range and mother and pup swim together towards it. The pup's stroke rate with his foreflippers is too high to be efficient. As he becomes used to diving he will learn to conserve energy.

At this depth the pressure is squeezing the flexible rib cage around his barrel chest. There is a tightening of his large lungs. The tiny air sacs in the extremities collapse and residual air is squeezed out of them, back into the larger airways, which are protected by a cartilage lining. Although there may be traces of nitrogen in the little bit of air left in the lungs, it is not absorbed.

A minute has passed since they left the surface. The sea bear knows to keep these first serious dives relatively short. While the pup rests, paddling just enough to keep himself steady, his mother noses about the sea floor in search of holes containing octopuses. Behind one outcrop she finds two ling, large-headed pinkish fish with tapered bodies, each about half a metre long. They are cruising along the bottom with eel-like undulations of their bodies. Their mission is similar to the sea bear's. They are searching for octopuses, although lobsters, squid and fish such as hoki will also satisfy them. Half-heartedly, the sea bear rushes at them and they accelerate away.

Now an octopus appears ahead of her, browsing the bottom for crabs and molluscs. It moves with a slow-motion rolling gait, its eight tentacles feeling for footholds and food. As the sea bear's threatening shape approaches, it transforms itself into something jet-propelled with metre-long arms trailing. At the same time, the octopus ejects a small cloud of ink and makes rapidly for the protection of a pile of boulders. Sinking into the spaces between them, it magically darkens itself for camouflage. Far from deterring the sea bear, the octopus's defensive ink cloud serves merely to excite her in the chase. With her pup close behind, she bores into the boulders with her snout, dislodging the small ones with thrusts of her powerful neck muscles. A little more fur comes away from her chin, which is already mostly bare, and some of her whiskers are a fraction shorter. She clamps on to one tentacle and rips it off the octopus. Still she quarries with frantic resolve. Her head and shoulders disappear in a second ejection of ink. Finally, she has the octopus in her jaws and dispatches it smartly. It becomes a floppy doll which mother and pup together devour, wrestling the prey from opposite directions.

Two minutes have now elapsed. For her pup's sake, the sea bear knows she must head for the surface soon. Swiftly the pair angle upwards, ignoring small schools of fish on the way. A human scuba diver ascending at this speed would risk nitrogen poisoning – the 'bends' – as bubbles of nitrogen in the bloodstream are released into nerve tissue and joints, causing severe pain, paralysis and, without decompression treatment, possibly death. Superbly adapted for deep dives through the way they regulate blood flow and oxygen uptake, sea lions avoid this condition.

Paafhhh! Poofhh! Two heads break the surface and begin inhaling. They take several deep breaths in quick succession, and the fresh air triggers physiological changes in reverse order. Heartbeat quickens, and with it the metabolic rate. Blood recirculates to the extremities, spreading warmth. Released from pressure, the blood that has pooled in sinus areas in organs such as the multi-lobed liver and kidney surges back into circulation.

Within five minutes the sea bear will coax her pup to forage again on the sea floor at even greater depths. On the bottom they will pursue again the pink-faced ling, slimy with mucus, and the darting jack mackerel, like miniature tuna, in mid-water. They will also encounter a fish the pup has not seen before, silver warehou, grey with a metallic sheen. It spawns in October. The pup will try excavating sea cucumbers from the bottom, and ingest round grey pebbles at the same time. The stones will lie in his stomach, an aid to digestion, until one day, while ashore, he will vomit them on to the coastal turf.

Before the hour is out he and his mother will dive two more times and after the second dive the sea bear will return to the surface with a ling too large to swallow or process on the sea floor. Then they will swim back to Enderby late in the evening, scramble over the lichen-white boulders with full stomachs and lie down in the tussocks within earshot of the ever-talking sea, which is their comfort, their sustenance, their element. Here they will stay for the next day and the day after that, with the pup occasionally helping himself to a top-up of mother's milk. But his suckling days are numbered. Before the month of October is out the sea bear will end the relationship. The next generation is swelling inside her. She is compelled to wean her pup of the year. If he has learnt the fishing techniques handed down over eons, he may get to challenge the Sandy Bay bulls several years hence, and perhaps assume the mantle of beachmaster.

THREE

BENEATH ITS WAVE-TOSSED SURFACE and far away from the crashing shores, the sea is an eloquent sound shell. It reverberates with the language and crisscrossing dialogue of beasts that have found communication in water more effective than in air. Water carries sound waves much farther – and five times more swiftly – than air. So much so that the low-frequency rumbles of whales may carry hundreds of kilometres through the sea. Silence is a stranger to the undersea world. From the scratch of crab legs on rock to the high-pitched echolocation clicks of the great whales, the ocean is a vast auditorium filled with sound.

Every time the sea bear enters it she expects her ears to tell her something about creatures in her immediate vicinity, whether other sea lions, whales or fish. Her ears are specially adapted to give her hearing in air as well as in water. The bones in them are sturdier than in land animals. Although waterborne sound waves reach her inner ear through the skull from all directions at once, she can distinguish the direction of sounds that matter to her, like those of other sea lions, just as readily as she can distinguish on land both the call of her pup and the direction from which it is coming. Underwater, the sea bear makes sounds varying from barks, grunts and growls to moans, squeals and clicks. She can hear sounds of much higher frequency than can humans, although many of the sounds are in undecipherable code, and the rapid-fire clicks of whales and dolphins – reaching 500 per second – go far beyond what she can hear let alone interpret.

Late October finds her swimming northeast of Enderby Island, following more or less her autumn and winter foraging tracks on the Auckland Islands Shelf. During those months, with a fast-growing pup to feed back on the island, she would begin her foraging dives while still close to land. During the course of the day, and still heading north or north-east, she would make six or seven dives an hour, lasting two or three minutes each. She would carry out these dives through the daylight hours and into the night. Darkness was not inhibiting for her. She worked extraordinarily hard. Now, well into spring, she continues her foraging north of Enderby but less energetically. She is feeding mainly to meet her own needs, including those of the developing foetus.

Enderby sea lions forage extensively across the Auckland Islands Shelf. This submerged shelf, up to 500 metres deep but mostly half that depth, forms a bump on the Campbell Plateau, which is a wide-ranging extension of continental shelf to the south and east of the New Zealand mainland. The Auckland Islands are located near the southwest edge of their shelf, and much of the sea lion foraging occurs on the relatively shallow waters to the north and north-east of the group, a region of high productivity. In particular, it is a prime habitat for arrow squid.

On her second dive of the day, the sea bear is listening out as usual for signals from other sea lions and anything that might suggest fish are in the vicinity. She does not often come upon other sea lions. A third of the way to the bottom, and with nothing in sight, she picks up a suspicious tingling through her whiskers. Her whiskers, richly supplied with nerves, perform as antennae. They are capable not only of helping measure speed through the water and temperature changes but also of sensing vibrations from prey and other creatures close by. Without these vibrissae the sea bear would be a much less successful predator. They are especially useful in the dark depths.

The tingling persists. She stops swimming and looks about her. She is confused. There are no fish to be seen; no give-away silver sides or bellies glinting in the dim light. As she is about to resume her dive, the tingling suddenly increases to a palpable vibration. She tenses, fully alert. Then she sees it – a large dark shape looming out of the depths, almost as long as a young whale but travelling much faster. Shark! A white shark, deadliest of all sharks, with 400 million years of ancestry as a predator to prove it.

The sea bear has seen such a shark only once before – after it had fed. Now she is staring at the enormous toothy gape of a white shark in attack mode and not ten metres away. She rolls and strikes out with frenzied foreflippers. Speed is her first thought. Then a swerving, jinking escape route. She is swimming faster than she has ever swum before.

The shark follows, mouth still wide open. His huge black eye, big as a saucer, is fastened on his quarry. But a white shark, for all its predator experience, does rely on the element of surprise to catch a sea lion and this time he is foiled by the sea bear's speed and agility – and the bristles around her mouth.

She swims at full speed for three minutes, angling gradually upwards, seeking solace in the light. With exhaustion setting in she surfaces, gasping. Head out of water, she cannot keep on guard against a further attack and soon begins porpoising steadily in a northerly direction.

Within half an hour she resumes her diving. Her practice is to make straight for the sea floor unless distracted by mid-water fish or squid. Then she will patrol a line of seabed for a minute or two before returning to the surface. In profile, her dives are bucket-shaped. Most are performed within the 250 metre contour but occasionally she goes deeper. She once descended over 400 metres. At such a depth the pressure is immense – some 40 times surface air pressure – and she was pushing physiological limits. It took her over ten minutes to complete the dive and 30 minutes to recover at the surface. Four hundred metres down, the ocean floor is as black as night. Here, she is more reliant than ever on her vibrissae to feel for food. Deep dives sometimes turn up schools of hoki, which are favoured eating. Like ling, hoki have tapered bodies and swim with a rippling movement. Their eyes are disproportionately large – the better to see with at depth – and their blue-green colouring blends well with the available light.

The sea bear does know some high spots on the shelf, less than 200 metres deep, where she can expect to find octopuses and bottom-dwelling fish. Her navigation aids include the relative positions of the sun and moon, the contours of the seabed and subtle changes in sea temperature. In the past she has made trips as far as the northern edge of the shelf. Beyond here the sea floor falls steeply to over 1,000 metres – depths well beyond sea lion capabilities. But shelf edges and slopes can act as giant food factories, and the sea bear associates the edges of the Auckland

Islands shelf with squid – an abundance of arrow squid.

Back in April she travelled far out on the shelf to feast on squid. She almost never came back. Her near-miss occurred one night after she picked up the sound of a motor vessel from a long way off – a large stern trawler. By the time she swam to the vicinity she could hear another raucous sound, that of winches grinding under the strain of a net heavy with arrow squid. The sea bear could see the squid, temptingly bundled in the cod end. She entered through the yawning net opening and began feasting on the squid, which at that time of year gather in huge numbers for spawning on the sea floor. Squid are handily packaged for a sea lion, with soft cylindrical cartilage-stiffened bodies weighing about a kilogram. The whole thing is digestible except for the mouth parts, which resemble a parrot's beak. Squid can be devoured on the spot, in three or four gulps. There is usually no need to process them at the surface.

By the time the sea bear has helped herself to several squid the net is on the point of being dragged up the stern of the vessel. The sides of the net crash against her, knocking her sideways. Her reaction is to swim upwards. She strikes the top of the net and bounces back. In wide-eyed panic, she heads for the front of the net. That way, too, is blocked, by a wall of squid. She smashes against the net again.

There is only one way out. She must swim towards the source of the awful noise. She clears the net just as the opening is about to be drawn up the vessel's stern ramp. The sea bear is one of the lucky ones. Dozens of her kind drown in the squid nets every year.

There are no squid trawlers on the shelf in spring. It will be February before they return, with their outlandish noise and foul-tasting discharges. The sea bear passes the place of trawler terror and pushes on. Night comes. She dives in the darkness and while coming up from the bottom encounters a school of same-sized slender tuna, about 70 centimetres long, feeding on krill. Their white undersides provide a target for her and she manages to seize one. She takes it to the surface to devour then rests the night out, drifting in the low swell. Hers is not a deep sleep. She dozes on her back, snout up, breathing at intervals.

By daybreak she has drifted north across the shelf edge. Feeling hungry, she dives and latches on to a school of barracouta feeding on krill. Over a metre long, they are fast fish with menacing canine teeth. The sea bear seizes one, and some of the krill for good measure. Suddenly she hears a sea lion sound, something between a grunt and a bark. Two sub-adult males appear. Boisterous four-year-olds, they too have been attracted by the barracouta. They make contact with the sea bear underwater, swimming around her and playfully grabbing at her hindflippers. All three animals surface and the circling, friendly contact continues for some minutes.

As suddenly as they appeared, the two males take off, heading north. They do not look back. The sea bear watches them porpoise away. It is a defining moment for her. She is as far north as she has ever been. Enderby is in the other direction. Enderby is what she knows. She knows nothing of the way north, the depth and character of the seabed, the taste and temperature of the water or what sort of food is available. Facing the sun, she grunts as if to reassure herself then explodes into life. She heads north. There is an old pathway through the sea.

PART V

Moturata

Instinctively
You know what the river is saying
Without being told.

BRIAN TURNER
'River Wind', 1989

ONE

TOWARDS DUSK on a cool November day, the purple kayak comes dancing down a riffle in the Taieri River. This is about the kayak's last chance to dance. Downstream the river widens and quietens for a smooth run across the Taieri Plain and through a coastal gorge to the sea. The kayaker enjoys the moment, dipping his paddle for steerage. His day on the river is about done. Before the light goes he wants to secure a camp site and fix himself dinner. His destination is the river's end – five or six hours' paddling from here in a sluggish current. He angles his craft towards a small clearing on the forested left bank of the river. He knows this place. In a few moments he has pulled the kayak ashore, through fringing kowhai and kanuka and into a glade of lemonwood and marbleleaf trees overtopped by kahikatea. He knows no one will disturb him here. The forest has swallowed him up, this man of the tussock country.

Still wearing the clothes he paddled in, including his Swanndri and denim cap, the Lark unpacks his little gas cooker and sets some river water to boil – exactly one and a half cups. He lays out a ground sheet and lightweight sleeping bag, and rigs a plastic fly to subcanopy branches. He cannot smell rain in the air but the afternoon clouds above the gorge suggested a roof over his head tonight might be a good idea. To the boiling water he adds a cup of white rice and turns the gas flame to low. It is a trusted recipe. In 12 minutes the rice is cooked, steamed dry. He saves some rice for breakfast and to the rest he adds a few slices of cold pre-cooked mutton and some red splashes of Tabasco sauce. Dinner is served and the cooker is reassigned to boil water for a brew of billy tea.

In the humid twilight of the forest, some bush birds – a pair of fluttering fantails and a lone tomtit – call at the camp looking for a supper of disturbed insects. The Lark obliges by scuffing up leaf litter and flicking grains of rice in their direction. There are tired lines across his face. It has been a long day. It started with a two-hour walk to the Strath Taieri turnaround point for the Dunedin-based Taieri Gorge tourist train, followed by a train ride as far as his kayak cache point, Hindon, then four hours on the river. He sloshes down his tea, removes his boots, rolls his jacket into a pillow and slides into the sleeping bag. Through the darkness, from both sides of the river, come the haunting calls – rhyming couplets – of moreporks, little native owls whose activity bodes well for a clear night.

Around dawn, birds of a different feather stir the Lark. Shining cuckoos, newly returned from wintering in tropical Western

Pacific islands, come drifting through the canopy in a noisy flock. In the next few weeks they will seek out grey warbler nests in which to lay their eggs. From his sleeping bag the Lark spots about a dozen of them jostling high above him. He recognises them not only from their trilling notes but also from the way the gathering light bounces off their metallic green feathers.

'And where were you when the shining cuckoos were calling?' he mutters to himself, remembering a Maori proverb on preparedness. He hauls himself out of the bag with a response: 'On the way to Taieri Mouth, that's where. For a look-see and a sea-look.'

It is his first trip to the Mouth since a visit in July during an uncommonly mild spell of weather. He has in mind to renew an acquaintance.

The journey continues through placid water, past the popular summer swimming spot of Outram Glen, past the township of Outram hidden behind high floodbanks and not yet properly awake, and on out into the flat cow country of the Taieri Plain. Here the river, barely above sea level, develops an intestinal-like meander. Canoeists of ancient times interpreted this serpentine path of the river as the twists and turns of a taniwha called Makamaka, which dug a tortuous track while searching dementedly for its lost master.

Beyond the track of the old water dragon the river straightens for its run past Henley, a Maori settlement site for generations past. It is all easy paddling as far as here. But as the Lark rounds the old pa site at Henley, passes under the 100-year-old Ferry Bridge and enters the river's last gorge, he feels the tug of the tide against him. In Humbug Reach, a gusty southwesterly conspires with the tide to challenge the paddler, prompting him to pull into John Bull Gully at the downstream end of the reach for a break, a brew and a bite to eat. It is already afternoon.

While waiting for the creek water to boil he takes a wander

through the gully where John Bull is said to have tended a potato patch in the silty soils. No spuds grow here now. The river, discoloured from lower Taieri sediment and swollen by the tide, is lapping the gully's grassy edge. The Lark knows high tide may mean he cannot camp at the cave at the Mouth, Tuckett's old cave. The alternatives include a night in the bush a short distance up the river or, if the conditions suit, he might book himself an island hideaway.

Relaunching his Pirouette after lunch, he startles two black shags from their whitened roosts on cliffs opposite the gully. Their presence reminds him to keep an eye out for falcons. In the Taieri Gorge, upstream of where he camped last night, he has seen a feisty falcon attack one of these shags, the largest of the New Zealand cormorants and four or five times the weight of the raptor.

The southwester funnelling down Humbug Reach is little more than a light breeze at the Mouth, and tending westerly. The Lark reaches his destination in mid-afternoon sunshine. He is keen to check out conditions. The purple kayak noses into the sand close to the Tuckett cave on the left bank downstream of the bridge. With the new-moon spring tide still making, the cave is at risk of flooding. The Lark leaves his craft here and walks down the lonely beach in bare feet, feeling the geological roots of Central Otago – schist sand, transported by river and sea – squelch between his toes. He passes George McIntosh's mighty macrocarpas and is soon inspecting some uneven diggings in the sand above the hightide mark – not the sand-castle workings of pre-schoolers but the wallows of a sea lion. There are fresh tracks leading seawards.

The Lark climbs a foredune to survey sea and surf – cool sibilant energy a world away from his usual haunts. The salt air is dense and sharp on his nostrils. Since last summer, he has mustered great inland seas of tussock and blade-shorn the sheep they nourished. He has installed new fences across dry and bony hills. At times, foot-sore and bothered by the heat, he has bathed himself in thoughts of this Taieri Mouth surf.

For more than ten minutes, sitting cross-legged in the marram grass, he gazes out over the surf and the humped backdrop of Moturata. He muses over the dynamics of river meeting sea – the cut and thrust of waves and currents. He studies the height, shape, break and run of the waves, and how many make a set. The swell is slight and the offshore breeze a restraining influence on the surf, whose lines are even and predictably spaced. Where the river thrusts past the island and a submerged sandbar to the north, the wave pattern is flattened. A gently rocking sea marks the river's destiny and death. For a river that has travelled more than 300 kilometres, death is shockingly swift.

Waves break to the right near the submerged sandbar. The Lark follows their track for a few minutes, assessing their suitability for a kayaker somewhat out of practice.

This is what he has come to see and feel. He has done as much seeing as he needs to. Now for the feel.

TWO

PADDLER, BARE FEET pressed into the foot plates, knees braced against the hull, body enveloped in neoprene splash skirt and waterproof jacket, arched forward, at one with the craft. Kayak outside the surf zone, heaving under the swells as if breathing with the sea. Count the waves in a set – four, sometimes five. For the easiest ride, take the first wave, usually the smallest. Kick start the kayak with a sweep stroke. Feel a responding surge – the kind of power that consumes a river.

Lean into the wave, trail the paddle in a rudder stroke. Kayak is taking off now. Lean and keep leaning. Dig that paddle in. Hold the line. Hold it. Keep in the green water, ahead of the curling, crumbling crest. Wave breaking. White water wreaths the cockpit – more froth than force at this point. Ride it, whooping, to the shallows.

THREE

HAVING SWAPPED his shepherd's Swanni for an anorak, with long-john woollens underneath, the Lark takes a few easy runs to start with. After each run down the right-breaking lines of surf north of the bar, he doubles back by slipstreaming on the river's path seaward. This avoids his having to break out through white water, although today the sea is about as gentle as it gets around here. A fishing boat rumbles towards the mouth, hardly pausing to check the wave pattern, confident of a smooth passage home.

He tries a bigger wave now and comes close to capsizing. This early in the season he is not keen on capsizing. Underwater, upside down but still locked into the cockpit, the paddler needs to execute an Eskimo roll to right the kayak. It is a technique that takes a lot of practice to perfect – the paddle angled up to the surface, with the body swinging in just the right manner, a flick of the hips and the head the last part to resurface.

Half an hour of catching waves is enough for the Lark. He disengages from the surf. As the lowering sun paints it a fluffy golden hue, he paddles steadily north outside the breaker line, parallel to the shore and close enough to be able to examine the string of sandy beaches stretching north to Kuri Bush. He is looking out for sea lions. The beaches are empty, however, as they usually are. Now Moturata beckons. He paddles back on a reciprocal course, making for a passage through a jumble of dark-brown rocks at the northern end of the island, the ocean side. Although the sea condition is a kayaker's dream, there is a surge to contend with around the rocks. He manoeuvres beam on to a flattish rock and uses the paddle, now behind him and braced against the rock, to hold the kayak steady while he heaves himself quickly backwards out of the cockpit and on to land. In virtually the same movement he has grabbed the kayak by the coving, the lip around the cockpit, and pulled it ashore.

The landing is a short distance from where he fancies spending the night – the half-formed sea cave with the water basin. His first thought is whether there will be a supply of fresh water, and he is reassured to see there is a healthy trickle emanating from under the overhang and filling the basin hollowed out in the rock. With the sun down now and dusk descending, he sets out his gear on the pebble floor of the overhang and prepares another meal. He has pasta in mind, enlivened with fried blue mussels gathered fresh from the tidal rocks. While the water is heating up he wanders off around the northern point to look for mussels in the ebbing tide, and to rediscover the jizz of the island, its character, its personality.

He is pretty certain he has the island to himself. The afternoon high tide will have stopped anyone crossing the tidal tongue of sand between the island and the mainland. Camped on the shady western side of the island, facing nothing but open sea, he is a willing castaway. Through the moonless night the sea rustles against the rocks.

Dawn comes calm. The Lark is conscious of aching muscles before he is aware of the weather. His arm muscles ache from the first surfing in months and even his thighs are sore from having to brace his legs against the hull. He stays in his bag longer than normal, his middle-aged frame relishing the comfort of a few branches of manuka slash between his ground sheet and the pebbles. Just on dark he borrowed the slash from the island's upper slopes. For the sake of the revegetation work going on up there he knows he must return the branches before he departs.

He wants to have a look around anyway, especially down the south end of the island – royal spoonbill breeding territory in the summer. Spoonbills are a novelty, strictly coastal birds. He never encounters them in the high country. He first came upon their nests on Moturata in the mid-1990s, just as they were establishing the colony here, on the western side of the island, out of view of Taieri Mouth people. He can relate to their sense of privacy.

By late-morning the Lark has had breakfast, redeposited the manuka slash and made contact with the spoonbills. Boulder-hopping his way back along the seaward shoreline, he rounds a rock arch and pauses. There is something different about the area up ahead where his kayak is parked. He senses company but no one is in sight. Then he sees it – a sea lion, hauled out on the rocks, its coat still wet and slick and dark enough to be that of a male.

'Brutus?' His voice nudges ahead of him.

'Is that you, fella?'

As the Lark approaches, the sea lion rises on its foreflippers, tips its head and snorts, mouth half open.

'Reckon it is you, you gadabout. Where ya been lately?'

The sea lion starts towards the Lark, revealing a left foreflipper with the two outer toe flaps missing. The Lark crouches and lets the animal, now positively identified, come up to him, rattling and scattering small rocks. With mouth wide open it half coughs, half roars at the Lark's face. His response is to extend a hand, gently, knuckle side forward. The sea lion quickly sniffs it then pulls back.

'Well, I'm a bit peckish, Brutus. Guess you'll have your own lunch organised.'

Crackers and cheese form the basis of the Lark's snack. While he eats he chats to the sea lion, now resting head-down. But the hint of an easterly breeze springing up is a signal to get on the move. He packs all his gear into the kayak. There will soon be no trace of his having camped here. He leaves till last exchanging his Swanni for the anorak.

The sea lion dozed through the Lark's lunch but is watchful now, eyes glistening.

'A seal launch would be appropriate, don't you think?'

Balancing the kayak on a smooth low rock close to the swirling water, he gets seated, secures the splash skirt and cradles the paddle across it. With arms either side of the craft he flattens his palms on the rock and shimmies forward. The kayak enters the water bow down but quickly rights itself as the back end scrapes its way clear of the rock.

Off to one side a furry torpedo slips into the water with the ease and elegance of a creature at home in the sea.

PART VI

New Frontier

> *Alone, alone, all, all alone*
> *Alone on a wide wide sea!*
>
> SAMUEL TAYLOR COLERIDGE
> 'The Rime of the Ancient Mariner', 1798

ONE

ON HER FOURTH DAY out from Enderby Island and now well north of the familiar feeding grounds of the Auckland Islands Shelf, the sea bear approaches a boundary. The sea's surface temperature has increased fractionally. She is beginning to see birds new to her. Having been unable to find the sea floor the previous day she dives now more out of exploration than hunger. She passes 300 metres and keeps going. At just under 400 metres she encounters the bottom, and impressive populations of squid and benthic fish. She has found the edge of the Snares Shelf, upon which The Snares group of islands is located.

For five minutes she explores the seabed, helping herself to a hoki on the way. In this region the shelf edge is curving. It straightens, like the shaft of the letter J, to take a northeast line all the way to the waters off Otago and the New Zealand mainland. It is a good place to be, and the sea bear knows it by the presence of so much marine life.

Two days later, still swimming north with assistance from the south-westerlies, she crosses another boundary but this one is different. It is the ocean equivalent of crossing a mountain range from a cool country to a warmer one. She feels a sudden increase in water temperature. In the space of just a few kilometres the seas to the north become a phenomenal two degrees warmer. She is crossing an oceanic front, the Subtropical Convergence. It is the meeting place of two vast water bodies – surface subantarctic water, which is driven north by south-west winds, and warmer subtropical water from the north. This front lassoes the entire Southern Ocean, with its wavy line following roughly the latitude of 45 degrees south. The sea bear pauses here on her journey. Squid are plentiful, and krill as well.

While resting at the surface at night, she hears fur seals barking. Sea bear and fur seals keep their distance. The sea bear has swum twice with them off the Auckland Islands during the fur seals' night-time feeding trips but she is not tempted to keep company with them here. She slumbers on.

In the morning she dives again, savouring the increased warmth. Her body is cleverly designed to maintain a blood temperature of 38 degrees Celsius even deep down in the sea where she might encounter temperatures as low as five degrees. Without fur, blubber and tricks of circulation, the cold water would suck the heat from her body. Her body is a sophisticated heat-exchange system. The network of veins and arteries through her flippers is so organised as to shunt blood away from the skin in the subantarctic seas. Conversely, to cool down on warm days ashore, she can pump blood through her flippers, which become radiators to be waved in the air. On sunny days at sea, after a strenuous dive, she may also wave a flipper in the air to cool down.

Her waterworks are also a marvel. Her kidneys are lumpy and highly efficient at desalination. Some of her fresh water requirements are supplied by prey, especially squid, which are mostly water. This water is extracted from the prey in an extraordinarily long small intestine, which can measure 22 metres.

The south-westerly winds that have accompanied her all the way from Enderby are fading now as a high-pressure weather system passes to the east of the South Island. North-east breezes have sprung up, opposing the south-west swell and building the waves. During her time at the surface she drifts west, and late in the afternoon of her sixth day she glimpses land to the west – Stewart Island. Birds are noticeably more plentiful. She meets rafts of sooty shearwaters as she porpoises towards the land, and parts them like a sheepdog through mustered sheep. At times, out of hunger, she dives in search of prey, and is surprised to find the shearwaters diving to where the light grows dim, about 20 metres down. Coming up under one raft of feeding muttonbirds, she nibbles at the dangling webbed feet. If pushed by hunger, she would eat a bird adrift on the sea but prefers scales to feathers.

Towards dusk she arrives at the land. Sea lion sounds, mixed with fur seal calls, guide her towards Ernest Island in the Port Pegasus area. She rounds a corner of the island to find three males in the water off a sandy beach and six more hauled out and passive on the sand. She utters a trilling sound under water and one of the males reacts by immediately rushing over to her. He is a six-year-old, excited by the arrival of a female into their midst. It is early November. Testosterone levels are rising. He tries shepherding the sea bear ashore. His mates join in. Jostled and now roaring defiance, she turns and swims quickly out of the bay, following the coast northwards until she reaches a quieter beach. She stands for a moment in the short surf, allowing her foreflippers to get used to her weight after eight days at sea. Then she waddles ashore and rolls in the sand. Over and over she rolls like a puppy in a sandpit. The sand is coarser and much warmer than Enderby's, and it is orange-tinged.

For the next two days, she rests. During the day she lies on the beach and flicks sand over her back as insulation against the higher daytime air temperatures at these latitudes. At night she prefers to lounge in dunes draped with the golden orange sand sedge, pingao, a coarser bed than the tussock grasses of Enderby.

At daybreak two days later, with the wind back in the southwest quarter and a three-metre swell charging up the east coast of Stewart Island, the sea bear returns to the water. The old pathway still pulls her north. Heavy showers dimple the waves and she raises her head to taste some of the rain, as if the rain were a reassuring element on a migration such as hers. When two fishing boats appear ahead of her she diverts eastwards to the open sea, troubled by their rumble, and only after their engine noise subsides does she head north again. On the horizon more land looms. The deep throb of a bulk carrier some kilometres distant causes her to alter course again for a time but she resumes a northeast track as it fades away.

By the evening she has closed on the coast again. There are fur seals in the vicinity. In addition, she is picking up patchy signals – squeaks and rapid clicks at the very limit of her hearing. Out of curiosity she moves towards the sounds. They are not the communications of whales but something else. As she enters a bay backed by a wide sweep of sand, a bay much broader than Sandy Bay, she finds the source of the clicks – dolphins. These are the petite Hector's dolphins of Porpoise Bay on the South Catlins Coast. From October to April they base themselves at the bay, often feeding in the surf on sprats or yellow-eyed mullet. A rocky arm projecting from South Head protects Porpoise Bay from southerly gales. Into this calm patch the sea bear follows a group of five dolphins, a family group. They are considerably smaller than her. They break the surface in turn with their rounded dorsal fins, a dark blade above a pale-grey back.

In the surf, responding to the energy of the waves, the dolphins become more active as they chase small fish. The sea bear tags along with them, swimming swiftly into and out of the surf, more intent on playing with these new creatures than with the pursuit of food – until she sees some wet-suited humans bobbing just outside the surf.

The dolphins weave among the humans, seemingly unafraid of them. But the sea bear is less sure of their intentions and steers clear. She breaks away altogether, heading for deeper water and a couple of spotted shags that have flown from cliff roost sites to check out the fishing in Porpoise Bay. The Hector's dolphins rarely scare them. A sea lion is a different matter. They take to the air in consternation, whacking the surface with their wings.

As darkness falls, the sea bear is on the move again. The coast immediately to the north is a series of brawny headlands, extending more eastwards than northwards. Towards midnight, with the Tautuku Peninsula light out to the left of her, the sea bear ceases swimming and drifts sleepily on a lessening swell, content to leave her journey in the hands of a fair breeze and a following current. Both propel her as assuredly as flippers if rather more slowly. For the breeze remains in the south-west, even if it is now fading, and the current is an ancient, enduring feature. It originates in the North Tasman Sea, conveying its residual subtropical warmth to the southern mainland regions of New Zealand – Stewart Island and the southern half of the South Island. This is the Southland Current. Having enveloped Stewart Island on its westward flow, it now hugs the Catlins Coast, insulating the land from the colder, saltier influence of subantarctic surface water.

At daybreak the sea bear is lolling off Purakaunui Bay. With the breeze having died away towards dawn, the ocean is a gently undulating waterbed. Inshore, near a line of cliffs white with lichen, the sea surface is disturbed by the frenzied feeding of slim young barracouta. Their metallic blue backs, topped by a sail-like forward dorsal fin, flash in the gathering light as they leap and criss-cross through a school of small fish.

The sea bear is suddenly hungry, suddenly energised. She porpoises towards the activity before descending to keep her presence a surprise. She snares a barracouta on the edge of the group and carries it transversely in her mouth with its head and tail thrashing. At the surface she quickly chomps it. As a result of the commotion, the other barracouta scatter, leaving the predator with little else to do but explore the sea floor. She makes a series of dives. Flounder and octopus inhabit these inshore waters where tracts of sand are interspersed with rock outcrops.

In this new, relatively warm environment the sea bear finds food in generous supply. Before long, she is lingering at depth more to satisfy curiosity than hunger. Even when she hears a motor while on the sea floor, she continues to explore. The noise increases then cuts out. While ascending for air she sees the hull of a launch about 30 metres off and drifting in the low swell.

'Poofhh!' She bursts above the sea and eyes up the vessel. There are voices. Two men. One of them disappears for a moment then is back in view holding something stick-like. He points it. Fires. The water beside the sea bear erupts. A roaring fills her head, many times louder than that of a lusty beachmaster. In an instant she turns and dives, terrified. A second shot strikes the water near her, a thunderclap that threatens to concuss her. Down, down she goes, down and away. Fleeing north, submerged. There is no looking back. Her kind has turned up on Purakaunui Beach before, shot through the head by people who regard sea lions and fur seals as competitors in the fishing grounds.

Ten kilometres north of the shooting incident is a favoured sea lion hauling ground – the adjacent beaches of Surat and Cannibal Bays, which are backed by an extensive area of marram-covered dunes. There are sea lion tracks and flattened marram grass throughout the dunes: sea lion city. In the waters off these bays the sea bear encounters her kind in ones and twos, all of them male, most of them less than six years old. They turn and tumble around her, clearly interested in the presence of a female even if, at their age, beachmaster status is merely fanciful.

She follows a couple of the Surat Bay residents for a distance as they head towards land, having been out feeding overnight. She draws close enough to the curving shore to make out several torpid bodies spread out on the sand. But she chooses not to haul out here. Through the rest of the morning she swims with the current, making a steady five knots. Passing Nugget Point she hears the underwater calls of fur seals in number and presses on, not caring to fraternise with them. The headland and its distinctive islets host a thriving colony of fur seals as well as, in sea caves hidden below the lighthouse, a handful of massive elephant seals of varying ages. Across broad Molyneux Bay she goes. Its sandy floor, a receptacle for sediments discharged by the Clutha River over eons, is a flatfish conurbation. Flounder, brill and sole occur here, large stocks of them. The shallow depths make diving easy and the sea bear eats her fill after rooting the camouflaged flatfish from their sand-snuggle. She misses the ones that have buried themselves so completely in the sand that only their upwards-pointing eyes protrude. The ones that try to escape, stirring the sand as they go, are easy pickings.

Although the river mouth is several kilometres away, she catches a taste of fresh water in the salt and a discoloration unlike anything she has experienced before. It is all very puzzling.

Lifting herself clear of the sea surface, she looks around for a sign of something awry. Nothing looks out of place. The land north of Molyneux Bay, however, is lower in profile, softer edged and less well forested.

Now the sea bear pauses on her journey, as if unsure of her orientation or where this migration is taking her. These waters are entirely new to her yet they carry way-marks such as temperature shifts, currents and the Clutha's freshness – way-marks that send an unconscious shimmer through her. Collectively, they are a code, the key to which lies deep within her, beyond any sort of conscious recognition. When unsure, a migratory being must pause. So she does, and for a few hours is content to float along on a lazy swell under a cool spring sky.

TWO

NORTH OF MOLYNEUX BAY the coast strikes a uniform northeast lie for 30 kilometres. Then another bay unfolds, more open than that of Molyneux. It, too, receives a river – the Taieri. Approaching from the south early next morning, the sea bear is prompted by the changing landscape and incipient hunger to check out the fishing in this wide bay. The sea floor is uneven here. There are holes deeply cut into the continental shelf, dark holes with craggy sides – hiding places for octopus, rock lobster and blue cod. She dives into one such hole and deep down surprises a small group of fat-lipped male blue cod that are distracted by a territorial dispute. Slate blue across their backs, with greenish sides, they attack each other with large pectoral fins whirring and their eyes moving independently. The sea bear ends the dispute by catching one of the adversaries and devouring him in the sunshine at the surface. Satisfied by the taste, she returns to the hole to find the blue cod dispersed and hiding, and resorts to foraging for what she knows best – octopus, in or out of a crevice.

As she swims away from the cod holes she encounters a freshness in the water, and a stain on the sea that is cloudier and browner than Molyneux's. The Taieri is in flood. With the shore close by, she is enticed to backtrack and explore the river mouth.

She sees an island disguising the mouth and enters the broad surf zone washing the sandy corner where the river bends north to meet the sea. It is an ample beach, wider than any in her experience. She rides a wave until it becomes a frothy ruffle. Then she stands and with hardly a sideways look marches boldly over an apron of wet hard sand till it becomes dry, soft and warm, and in the late-morning sun as white as her belly. She squints in the brightness, flops down and rolls one way then the other, then back again. For the moment she is a land animal, seemingly engaged in a ritual reconnection with the earth.

The beach is deserted except for a pair of black oystercatchers that seek out sand hoppers and other invertebrate food in clumps of stranded bladder kelp. They work urgently with bills longer than their legs. They have produced eggs already, three of them, lying like smooth speckled rocks in a shallow scrape of sand above the high tide mark. If the sea bear approaches the nest, the pair will let her know with their shrill 'kleep-kleep-kleep-kleep' calls, and one bird will drag a wing, feigning injury to try to entice the intruder away. Dotted along the beach are pieces of driftwood, some large and multi-limbed and still carrying vestiges of foliage, some as bleached and polished as river-rolled rocks. The river itself, flowing swiftly with the ebbing tide, is flood-brown.

Thirty minutes after leaving the water the sea bear shuffles into the marram-clad foredunes behind the beach. Her tracks in the sand are deep and distinctive, sickle-shaped like a giant turtle's. She meanders through the dunes as if looking for something – as if she has been here before. Again she rests for a short time then is drawn back to the beach and the water. She launches into the waves and strikes out north-east towards the hills in the distance but with a memory now of Taieri Mouth, its quiet dunes and bountiful fishing holes.

And still, the pull is to the north. The coastline ahead curves towards a high dark knuckle of land, the volcanic hills of Dunedin and Otago Peninsula. By the end of the day she has passed Dunedin City's main beaches without being aware of them, and closed on the southern shores of Otago Peninsula, where basalt cliffs, some of them over 200 metres high, meet the Pacific Ocean.

Over the years southerly gales have shorn the trees and shrubs on the cliff tops and blasted sand from the beaches hundreds of metres inland. Sandfly Bay is backed by vast sand drifts, a Saharan landscape. Here the sand really does fly, reaching Sandymount at over 300 metres above sea level. This soaring sand imprint is visible from Nugget Point on a clear day. Below Sandymount, waves of terrible power and persistence have hollowed out caves at the base of the cliffs. Once huge caverns, the two largest sea caves along this coast collapsed long ago to reveal sheer or overhanging sides decorated with rock columns not unlike those found on the basalt cliffs of the Auckland Islands. How many sea lions migrating from the subantarctic region have skirted these places in the way the sea bear is now doing? She porpoises through a placid sea with new-found certainty. She seems to know where she is going.

Contact with a southern right whale half a kilometre off the cliffs of Sandymount – the first whale she has encountered since leaving Port Ross some three weeks earlier – serves to reinforce her certainty. She skirts around the whale, yelping playfully. The whale lumbers on, unresponsive. Sea birds dot the sky out to the horizon, among them skimming prions and squadrons of Stewart

Island shags. A lone royal albatross tracks north. In the light winds it must flap more than glide. No doubt it is bound for its colony at Taiaroa Head, the tip of Otago Peninsula. Superb navigators, the royals of Taiaroa come home every second year after travelling right around the Southern Ocean.

As for the sea bear, she has Cape Saunders in her sights now – the Peninsula's eastern promontory. Little visited by people, it is a bleak and bony headland, carrying one of the few names left by James Cook on this part of the coast. From here, the land bends north past private Papanui Beach and soon opens up a three-kilometre stretch of sand, the peninsula's longest beach. Ever so gently curved, Victory Beach guards a shallow inlet of the sea, Papanui Inlet. At the southern end of the beach is the inlet's channel, well sheltered from southerly weather, and nearby, forming a dark backdrop on the foredunes, is a plantation of the ubiquitous radiata pine, like macrocarpa an import from California. Backing the rest of the beach is a broad apron of dune slack and coastal turf, a wildlife reserve.

Into this secluded setting, towards evening, surfs the sea bear. Her long journey from Enderby Island is over. This haul-out site is the northernmost regularly used by the species. It is a new frontier. Like many a frontier in the world of seals, it has been forged by males. The arrival of a female is a momentous thing. But the moment is lost on the resident males. Two males aged four and six lie motionless on the sand near the entrance to the inlet, sound asleep; three other youngsters, also male, are flattening the marram grass on the short spit overlooking the channel. All is quiet except for the rhythmic wash of surf on a shelving beach.

The sea bear glides in past a rusty old flywheel embedded in the surf zone – a relic from the 1861 wreck of the steamship *Victory* – and makes her acquaintance with Victory Beach. Exuberantly, she rolls in the sand then slumps down in it. Although the warmest part of the day is over and she has no need to insulate herself from the sun's heat, she begins flicking sand across her back, using her foreflippers in turn until she looks more like a mound of sand than a sea lion. She sleeps the deep sleep of a long-distance traveller.

As night falls, and still unrecognised by the beach's male incumbents, she climbs the steep foredune on unsteady limbs to investigate the dim interior of the pine plantation. The plantation is a comfort to her. It mimics the forest fringes of the haul-out sites in her subantarctic homeland. Virtually nothing grows within it except for thickets of elderberry in the light wells of firebreaks. Pine needles lie mattress deep on the forest floor. She wanders purposefully into the pines, following an avenue and stopping only to scent the air and defecate. Her droppings are like those of a large dog and she leaves them uncovered. About 50 metres into the pines she suddenly stops and stretches out on the bed of needles, chin and flippers flattened. She flicks a few needles over her back and, still puffing at intervals from the exertion of life on land, she closes her eyes.

This place is a long way from Enderby Island. Cool, comfortable and within earshot of the surf, Victory Beach is a haven for a sea lion at the end of a migration. She rests easy.

Through the next day she sleeps, then on the following morning a sharp abdominal pain wakes her. It is a labour pain, although six weeks too early. She reacts by lifting her head and bending around to inspect her abdomen. She is confused. She sets out for a place of solace, the sea. The twinges keep coming. She breaks out of the plantation and stumbles through the marram. Near the upper edge of the beach, where the grass thins out, she halts and bellows as another spasm hits her. The pup is coming, flippers first and taking its time. Finally it is expelled. But something is wrong. It is not moving. The sea bear licks it and nudges it with her nose. For about ten minutes she tries to rouse the pup, unable to accept it is still-born.

She stays with the lifeless brown pile all day. Two of the hauled-out males leave for sea and a new male turns up, his dark-brown coat glistening as he ambles shore. None of these animals is aware of the sea bear's presence in the marram.

During the afternoon a southwest front hits the Peninsula, darkening the sky and producing a series of squalls. The creamy sand turns brown and sodden with the spring rain, and the temperature plummets 10 degrees within half an hour. In the evening, with hunger mounting, the sea bear makes for the water. At the surf she meets a returning resident male, a six-year-old. He approaches the sea bear, swimming powerfully across the waves to cut her off then wading the last few metres to make himself taller than her. He challenges with an open-mouthed roar. She roars in response. For a few moments they stand in the chest-high surf, eyeing each other. The sea bear is in no mood to continue the exchange, however. She sidesteps him, plunges seaward and is quickly swallowed up by the darkening sea and sky.

Through the night the sea bear explores the feeding grounds off Victory Beach and readily satisfies her hunger. First, not far from shore, she surprises a small group of banded wrasse at a reef bedecked with seaweed, and swallows two of them whole. Farther out, in deeper water, she catches a red cod. These grounds are new to her and she dives frequently to the seabed of the continental shelf to check out the fishing prospects. She detects octopus in numbers.

At about 15 kilometres out, the sea floor falls sharply away. She has found the head of Papanui Canyon, one of several high-walled canyons that project deep dark fingers towards the Peninsula – handy supermarkets for fur seals and sea lions. The canyons, reaching depths of about 800 metres, are connected to an enormous submarine valley far out to sea. At a depth of about 150 metres the sea bear comes upon several elephant fish half a metre in length. She snares one and carries it to the surface to eat. It is a cartilaginous fish, with no bones or scales – a delicious meal.

Through the remainder of the night she lazes. She has discovered the edge of the continental shelf and will remember its location on future fishing trips. Lolling at the surface, she is passed by a number of fur seals. They keep their distance. Before the sky begins to lighten on the watery horizon she is heading back to Victory Beach.

THREE

IN THE NEXT WEEKS the sea bear will forage in the canyons and on the continental shelf off Otago Peninsula. Mostly she will swim beyond the normal foraging range of the male sea lions. In the course of exploring the area she will discover a second main hauling ground, around the corner at Papanui Beach. Again she is the only female on the beach. Papanui has a narrower set of dunes and the males are grouped more closely, often in groups of three or four, asleep with skins touching and sometimes a flipper draped over the next animal.

By mid-December the sea bear has made herself at home at Victory Beach. She, more than the males, uses the pines as a rest site, mostly out of choice but also, increasingly, to escape the males' breeding instincts. They now, singly or in number, try to intercept and herd her on the sand. The oldest males have disappeared to places unknown. One or two may even travel as far as the Auckland Islands, from where they no doubt migrated, to battle it out with the beachmasters. They will not be back till February, and some will carry wounds. Then one day the sea bear, too, is gone from Victory Beach.

She heads south at a steady pace, passing Saunders, Sandymount and the tombolo that forms the city beaches and connects Otago Peninsula to the mainland. On past Brighton she goes but her track is slowly closing with the land. On the north side of Taieri Mouth, she leaves the sea and roams the shrubby dunes distractedly – the dunes she explored on her way north. It is as if she is answering the call to give birth. For the next few days she is based here, feeding mostly at night and returning after dawn. While on the beach one still morning, hunkered down and tired from energetic foraging, she is approached by a man and a dog. With her left eye she watches the two of them, motionless. The other eye is closed. A cataract is slowly developing in it. In years to come it will spread a pale mask across the iris, inhibiting her vision. Flies buzz about her open eye, attracted by the tears that stain the fur below it.

In the afternoon other men approach her at her sand wallow. She has scarcely moved. One of them approaches a metre too close to her and she lifts and turns, not knowing that in such a simple movement she gives away her identity through revealing the little circular tag on her right foreflipper.

The summer solstice passes. There is no pup, and never can be this summer. No males to mate with, either.

Subtle in the way they manifest, the sea bear's reproductive hormones finally coax her to seek out a mate. She leaves Taieri Mouth, its cloistered dunes, landmark island and profitable cod holes, and heads south once more. Surat Bay is her reference point. Across Molyneux Bay and around Nugget Point she steers, swimming through the night and half the next day, porpoising with purpose. False Islet confuses her navigation, especially as there is a good sea running, towed along by a stiff southerly which is blowing the white caps to spume. But she knows she is in the vicinity of the hauling ground and is soon riding the breakers ashore at

Surat Bay, another beach named after a 19th century shipwreck.

The big boys of Surat Bay have also moved away, leaving the beach to a few young bachelor bulls. At first glance they might easily mistake her for a male rising two years of age, for her colouring is not unlike that of males in their first year or two. A second glance might tell them otherwise – and it does. When the sea bear wanders amongst them she soon gets attention. The arrival of a female in season is a call to battle.

Two subadults, three and four years old, stride up to her, heads swaying, mouths open as they roar their calling cards. The commotion stirs a six-year-old lying close to the dunes – a bull with a rich brown coat, which carries no sign yet of a silvery beachmaster mane. Bigger and deeper-voiced than the other two, he challenges them for the cow and after several minutes of skirmishing succeeds in placing himself between them and her. Backed up towards the water, the sea bear does not flee into the surf but rather waits for the fighting to die down and for her champion to mate with her.

She stays at Surat Bay for two days, closely attended by the six-year-old. He brooks no rivals, and mounts her several times.

On the third day, despite the best efforts of the subadult sire to detain her, she makes for the surf and is soon rounding False Islet, heading north. This time she does not call at Taieri Mouth. Except for some feeding en route she heads straight back to Otago Peninsula and her new-found home at Victory Beach.

She is no longer a migrant. She is a colonist now. As the first resident female, she has a critical role. She is a matriarch in the making.

PART VII

The Mouth Revisited

> *I hope one day they'll plant me in*
>
> *The kind of hole they dig for horses*
> *Under a hilltop cabbage tree*
>
> *Not too far from the river that goes*
> *Southwards to the always talking sea*
>
> JAMES K. BAXTER
> 'At Kuri Bush', 1966

ONE

THERE IS A WINTRY DRIP at the end of my nose. It is one of those days – nose-dripping, eye-watering, ear-tingling. A chill westerly dominates the day, a wind of subantarctic character, shepherding greyish clouds across a blue canvas of sky and biting away at exposed skin and any weak point in your clothing. Here at Taieri Mouth in mid-July the day is unsure whether to stay fine or turn bleak all of a sudden. Regardless, the breakers march towards the sandbar connecting mainland and island with an evenness that seems unnatural and a wispy bouffant hairdo courtesy of the wind.

I brush a drip from my nose. I am reminded of Janet Frame's poem, *Sunday Afternoon at Two O'clock*, about 1960s life in Dunedin on the Sabbath, in which she describes the local church-goers as having 'sober drops at the end of their cold Dunedin noses'. This is not Sunday afternoon but Thursday morning and Martin Palmer, ever reliable and well rugged up, is waiting at the mainland end of the sand bar with his red, fat-tyred Kawasaki four-wheeler, which is pointed at the island, Moturata, and ready to whisk me over there. I have not seen him in at least 12 months. He extends a sturdy hand, pocket-warmed.

'We'd better be getting on the way,' he says. 'Tide's on the make but we'll have a good hour on the island.'

I had phoned him earlier in the morning from my Otago Peninsula home to check on the state of the bar and tide, and ask whether he thought the conditions okay for walking to the island. I wanted to see how the island revegetation project was going and how the plants had fared after a distressingly dry summer. I also thought I'd keep an eye out for sea lions. Martin insisted on transporting me on his four-wheeler.

'You'll have more time that way. Safer, too. I wouldn't trust the tide walking over just now.'

And so we rendezvous where the sand bar meets the mainland dunes, beside the sluggish Taieri, recovered now from a summer of record low flows and temperatures uncomfortably high for fish and other life. The four-wheeler is really a wide motorbike made for rough terrain and stable even with a pillion passenger. I pull my woollen hat lower over my ears, zip and button up my windproof jacket and hop on. Across the sand we go, dodging around a mosaic of pools and channels – the sea's signature. There are two such scrolls a day, each different in the marks it leaves. We splash through sea water in the deepest of the channels, causing me to wonder whether the making tide will reclaim it before we return. From sea level the breakers appear massive rolling towards us, and the sea beyond, penguin blue, is white-flecked and clearly in a disturbed mood.

The bar extends more than a kilometre, forcing the river to exit to the north of the island. We reach it in about five minutes. On arrival Martin checks in his pockets for something. He pulls out a mobile phone.

'A back-up,' he says. 'In case we get stuck on the island. There's the odd freak wave, that sort of thing.'

The last time we were here, a fishing boat dropped us off and Martin very nearly got swept away trying to wade through thigh-deep water. This time our feet are dry and we scramble up a crumbly bank at the northern end, the site of the old Maori burial ground. It is also an access way for penguins. Myriad claw marks are etched into the baked clay, testimony to the climbing prowess, not to mention determination, of these birds.

On the flat area above is a sight that gives Martin and his island helpers much pleasure – plant life proliferating. The eradication of rabbits has made all the difference.

Carpets of tufted manuka are spreading out from branches laid to halt the desertification. Rounded shrubs of *Hebe elliptica*, planted in groves, are about twice the height they were when I was last here. Coastal plants, they thrive in salt winds and seem to put on new foliage all year round. Right now, in the depths of winter, these juvenile shore hebes are looking a picture. Also doing well are the transplanted flax and toetoe, and clumps of orange sand-binding pingao.

Martin leads the way farther up the island. We pass a collection of holes angling into the dark earth – burrows. Judging by the loosened soil at their entrances, they are currently occupied.

'Penguins or shearwaters?' I ask.

'Not sure. Could be either – or both. But titi are usually the boss. I've seen them come in at dusk and kick out the resident penguins. You should hear them carry on. It's a real scrap.'

We push on up to the island's high point where Martin hopes his young rata trees will one day fly their red flowers like flags to commemorate the island's ancient name, Moturata, Rata Island. Only two of the five seedling trees have survived in the clearing in the flax but they are looking vigorous enough.

'You know, some people wonder why we're going to all this trouble,' he says. 'They think the island should be left to its own devices, to blow itself to bits till the soil is stripped and only the rocks are left. But – God's sakes – my grandfather and great-grandfather knew this place, and what would they think if my generation let it go to the pack? It's heritage. We need to make the effort.'

Martin is about as stirred up as I've seen him.

'You must be pretty chuffed with the result.'

'Well, we've had some help all right. Lots of people. During the drought last summer friends of the island even carted containers of fresh water out here to keep the plants going.' Martin pauses for a moment. 'Then again, maybe the "little lady" had something to do with it, too.'

'Little lady?"

'The kuia we reburied here. She lived over 200 years ago. You might remember – I mentioned it when you were last here – her bones were uncovered by erosion.'

I nod. 'Go on.'

'Well, we wanted her reburied with a proper ceremony before we started the replanting work. And you know, things never looked back. They reckon even the fishing got better after that. Speaking of the sea, we'd better get going.'

The wind nips at our faces as we retrace our steps. Most of the revegetation work has focussed on the slopes exposed to the westerly and southerly winds. When I ask about the wooded ocean side of the island, Martin mentions the spoonbills and how they have been roosting and nesting in the trees over the summer. I make a note to come back in late spring to check on whether they are nesting. I have seen them on Green Island, north of Brighton, nesting in taupata, the big coprosma trees. There, too, they favoured the ocean side of the island for nesting, obscured from the mainland, away from public gaze.

Crossing the flat area again, above the old burial ground, I feel something invisible tugging at me, a memory jog.

'Isn't there an old stone hearth here somewhere, Martin?'

'You're right. This is the place all right. Over here, look.'

He pulls away a mat of manuka to expose a flat stone on its edge, a corner of the hearth. We saw it last time. It did not occur to me then but I now realise some of the island's pre-European occupants would have been camping and cooking within a few metres of an urupa.

'Isn't that an unusual thing – cooking close to a burial site?' I say.

'Yes, we've wondered about that, too. Could be the island was occupied in later times by people who were unaware of the urupa. There are layers of occupation here, with several generations separating some of them.'

As we make our way back to the four-wheeler, I speculate on what archaeologists a hundred years from now will stumble on as a result of the revegetation project – notably the grids of rusting number eight wire used to tie down the manuka brush.

Back on the island's sandy apron, Martin dips his hands in a pool of sea water left by the outgoing tide. This is his practice upon leaving the island and its burial ground. It is a mark of respect for the ancestral dead.

There are still anglers, on foot, fishing the river from the sand bar so I know we are not too late getting back. At the Palmer house overlooking the mouth, bar and island, Martin's wife, Barbara, has prepared a hearty, warming lunch. The conversation comes round to my trip south for sea lion work, and I ask whether there have been any sightings lately at the Mouth.

'All quiet,' says Martin. 'But did you hear Mum was back over Christmas?'

'Another pup – yes, I did know. She's getting quite a reputation.'

'We've only ever had one or two sea lions at a time here. First one I remember ever seeing was camped behind Taieri Beach. That must have been back in the 1950s.

'Caused a ruckus round here, I tell you. She was big and dark brown and – '

'More likely a he than a she,' I cut in.

'Well, anyway, local people learned to give this big bloke a wide berth. He had a camping spot in the lupins, and when he wasn't there we'd go and have a look at it. Used to see bits of broken shell from crayfish bodies lying about the nest. That stirred up the locals, I tell you, seeing cray remains.'

Talk of campsites puts me in mind of the cave down by the river, near George McIntosh's place, where I met the Lark. There might be time to check it out before the tide is fully in, so I take my leave of the Palmers and drive down to the river. By the bridge is a new sign for visitors. Taieri Mouth recently joined the great Southern Scenic Route, a tourist promotion connecting it with the likes of Nugget Point and Waikawa and all the way round to Te Anau and Milford Sound. The new sign features a map with landmarks and attractions, all of it drawn by hand. None of your corporate logo stuff here. It has character. It sums up Moturata this way: 'Sanctuary for Sooty shearwater, Blue penguins, Black shag, Gulls, Seals and the odd Sea Lion.'

'Odd', as in 'occasional', or 'odd' as in 'strange'? If Mum is the sea lion the signwriters had in mind, they could have thrown in 'quirky', 'clever', 'one out of the box'.

On the north side of the river now, I scramble down a bank and walk along the beach towards the cave. The tide is well in. Frothing tongues of the advancing tide slap against a bluff, forestalling me. I can see the cave in the distance. No one is there.

Back on the road and around the corner, I call at the McIntosh home. Again, no one at home. But, inside, a radio is blaring. Perhaps George is out the back. I walk around to the garden shed. Still no one. And no car. Perhaps those cunning Oriental cats turned on the radio? From here, there is a wonderful view of the island, and with my eye I trace the meanderings of Martin and I across it earlier in the day. Then I notice a movement at the foot of the island's northern cliffs. There is a person, just the one, I think, standing beside what appears to be a canoe or kayak. It is a dark colour. Is it deep purple? Could it be the Lark, back from the high country?

TWO

COMPARED TO TAIERI MOUTH and its sporadic experience of sea lions, Dunedin is sea lion city. The main sea lion haul-out sites, on Otago Peninsula, are well within city limits, although off the beaten track. Few local people ever get to see them, except when the media lock on to the antics of young extrovert males. Acting alone, they do the darndest things and a front-page picture or a television appearance is often the result.

Like the time when a sea lion came ashore at St Clair Beach, climbed the concrete steps to the Esplanade, crossed the road, marched through the front gate of a seaside home and camped intimidatingly at the resident's back door. This went on for days, with the sea lion coming and going several times. Then there was the young male, a different animal, that hauled out at St Kilda Beach, just up the way from St Clair, and entertained large crowds of people by lunging at the wheels of cars moving along John Wilson Memorial Drive. In Otago Harbour, individual sea lions are occasionally photographed with a flounder or salmon in their mouths. One adventurer unwittingly – or wittingly? – taunted salmon anglers fishing off the wharves at the head of the harbour by devouring a trophy-sized salmon at the surface right in front of them. Sometimes these harbour visitors use a slipway for resting on; sometimes they remain in the water and scare the daylights out of rowers and windsurfers with their bravado and the size of their fangs. When they become a nuisance on land Department of Conservation officers turn up waving big sticks. The bamboo poles are used not for beating the sea lion but for herding it back into the water. Always the public message is the same: give sea lions a wide berth and back off if they approach.

Which makes the work of marine scientist Chris Lalas rather special. He and post-grad students like Shaun McConkey have spent a huge amount of time getting close up to the Otago sea lions in order to study population dynamics, movements between haul-out sites, social behaviour and diet. For years Chris has painstakingly compiled diet information, the first of its kind, season by season. Because there are few dead animals to autopsy and stomach pumping of live animals is hardly an option, he has to collect faeces and vomit material if he wants to know what the sea lions eat. He targets sea lion wallows and tracks, and sometimes snatches the doings from right beside a sleeping animal. Once in the bag, the material is sieved for indigestible traces of prey. This often takes the form of the hard beaks of squid and octopus or the bony part of the inner ear, called the otolith, which differs from fish species to fish species and provides an accurate clue to the type of prey.

Sea lion movement studies rely on identifying individuals. In the days before the scientists could name most of the Peninsula animals through features such as warts, scars and other marks, they used spray paint as a temporary tagging measure. The paint – different colours placed on different parts of the animal – lasted about a month. It was certainly all gone after the sea lion moulted.

But first you had to apply the paint. This involved close quarters stuff – sneaking up to the sea lion to be tagged and squirting on paint from an aerosol can. Chris Lalas was well practised at it. I have seen him kneel on the sand in front of a large young male, virtually eyeball to eyeball, and sway backwards as the sea lion roared defiantly in his face, centimetres away. When it was the animal's turn to sway back on its haunches, Chris would lean forward and spray a foreflipper before retreating. Just watching such a show could put your heart in your mouth.

On these expeditions I would ask Chris, 'How do you know whether they mean to say hello or bite your head off? Can you distinguish between bluff and belligerence?' And Chris would say, yes, he did know when an animal meant business, but that instinctive sort of understanding came only as a result of long years of relating to sea lions.

Mum was a different experience altogether. Mum was a honey. She was about as placid and accepting as a sea lion could get, except around pupping time. In the spring of 1991, when Chris Lalas first recorded her presence on Otago Peninsula, she was the only female then resident on the Peninsula. The researchers had a number for her but no name. Her name came later. On her right flipper was a small yellow tag, which confirmed her Enderby Island origins. Around Christmas 1993, she created history at Taieri Mouth, producing the first sea lion pup recorded on mainland New Zealand in modern times. By now she had lost her tag – it had been ripped out through the loose skin of her flipper, perhaps by becoming snagged on something. Still, the researchers recognised her. The fleshy tip of her right big toe was distinctively blunt, as if it had been chewed off square or simply grown that way. She also had something wrong with her right eye, possibly the beginnings of a cataract.

Of compelling interest was her selection of the Taieri Mouth dunes as a nursery site ahead of the Otago Peninsula beaches. What drew her there? Perhaps it was the isolation from hassling males. That and good fishing grounds not too far from shore. Back on Victory Beach she would have had ten to 20 young males for company and their efforts to mate with her would almost certainly have caused problems for her pup. To the delight of the scientists the pioneering pup was female and from then on its mother was known as Mum. Of course, a single pup does not a colony make. But two years later, having missed a breeding season through her separation from potential mates, Mum again turned up at Taieri Mouth and gave birth to another female pup. Two years on, again at Taieri Mouth, she produced a third pup, also female.

Chris Lalas and his colleagues were amazed – a run of female pups joining a population drastically short of females. Taieri Mouth people who had taken an interest in Mum from the start claimed her as their own, proud as grandparents. All healthy, the pups were faithfully escorted back to Victory Beach by Mum within a couple of months.

Questions surrounded this wildlife phenomenon. Were we seeing the start of sea lion recolonisation on the mainland? Did Mum, as if to order, produce a string of female pups to compensate for the gender imbalance at this new frontier? Or was it just a fluke?

In the course of their various studies, the researchers recorded Mum's movements. At Victory Beach she favoured holing up in the pines rather than in the marram grass with most of the males. Early in September of 1997 Chris, Shaun and I caught up with her in the plantation. She was resting, half-asleep in the dappled light, with her second pup, Leone, close by. Leone approached and sniffed us before shuffling back to her mother's side. Mum barely raised her head from her bed of pine needles. She was breathing loudly at intervals with her good eye upwards. Then, probably more to comfort her rotund pup than to provide a feed, she rolled over to expose her nipples. Leone suckled. It was a rare sight – a 20-month-old pup not yet weaned.

THREE

THE TIDES are a kind of breathing – in, out, flood, ebb, forever alternating to a lunar rhythm. The moon – and the sun to a lesser degree – draws the sea sluggishly towards it, causing the sea to bulge where the moon is located over the earth and sea levels to rise and fall accordingly. No two tides are the same in their reach, their wave pattern or their impact on shifting sands. For the breathing is at full stretch at spring tides and more softly expressed at the neaps. Adding to the variation, storms out to sea increase the flood tide's impact on the land. Two weeks separate the spring tides (full moon and new moon). Neap tides fill the weeks between. Tides wait for no man, least of all a birdwatcher busting to get to a tide island on foot.

I fancy catching up with the royal spoonbills on Moturata, and the idea of walking to their nesting area is appealing. You cannot ordinarily do this because on the east coast of the South Island the spoonbills breed on islands through spring and summer. Moturata is not as private as they might imagine, though. Most days, when the sand bar is well consolidated, the island is accessible on foot one to two hours before low tide. Knowing there ought to be eggs and very probably chicks by late November, I select a mid-morning low tide only to find it is a neap and that the sea is drawing too little breath for my liking. The tide is not out far enough; the bar is menacingly narrow.

Eight days later there is a spring tide – a king tide, as I have heard anglers call it. The complementary low spring tide is really low, exposing a tract of sand many times wider than the river. Okay, spoonbills: here I come, Red Band gumboots and all, ready or not. I set out on foot around noon. It seems sensible to follow the winding edge of the river on my left, half a figure eight. The river is a comfort, more of a known quantity than the sea, which presents a low white blur of breaker lines. They seem to stretch to the horizon. An easterly breeze is puffing up off the sea, chilling the air on a day that is clear and trying its best to substantiate the onset of summer. I have a fair idea where the spoonbills will be – on the ocean side of the island, towards the south end. I aim to creep up on them. Having seen how sensitive the Green Island spoonbills are, I know these ones are likely to take to the air at the sight or sound of anything untoward.

As colonisers, royal spoonbills have the jump on sea lions. Maukiekie, off Moeraki Peninsula, and Green Island were colonised in the 1980s and nests were found on Moturata for the first time in the mid-1990s. They are gradually leapfrogging their way south. An islet off Nugget Point has also hosted breeding spoonbills. They are moderately-large heron-like birds, standing over 70 centimetres tall and as snow white as kotuku. The bill is of bizarre design, a long black extension of a black face and spoon-shaped near the tip. But it does the job. Spoonbills feed on estuaries, using their remarkable bills to sweep the mudflats in a side-to-side arcing fashion in search of invertebrate life and small fish. They operate as much by touch as by sight, it seems, for they feed during darkness as well as in daylight. Maori have a descriptive name for the birds – kotuku ngutupapa, flat-mouthed white herons. From winter feeding grounds in the north they return in spring to build nests of sticks woven into the upper branches of trees handy to water. On Green Island they use taupata trees; on Moturata large old *Hebe elliptica* provide habitat.

And there they are – a scattering of white blobs in the dark green canopy. Binoculars reveal delicate nuptial plumes. One pair, late breeders perhaps, are engaged in a display of bowing and bill clappering that marks the pair bonding period. Maybe they are still expecting eggs.

I edge forward with camera and long lens at the ready, feeling somewhat exposed. How many black faces have me in view? I soon get an answer. One bird lifts off and within moments the rest have joined it – a good dozen birds. They drift into a line and head out to sea a way before turning to the north. They circle above the island then I lose sight of them. Disappointed at their timidity, I know there is little point in observing them at their nests without a hide and begin retracing my steps.

Back at the island's northern end I am now facing the McIntosh sand dunes on the opposite side of the river. I should call on George and ask if he has seen anything of Mum, whom we encountered here about this time a year ago. She came wandering through the dunes as if inspecting an old stamping ground. She was in good condition – either pregnant or very well fed. For about half an hour Mum roamed the dunes and occasionally she would stop and swivel round to touch her rear end. We thought she might be experiencing labour pains. She disappeared to sea in the evening and turned up a week or two later to have her pup. This time she swam upstream about a kilometre, just past the Tuckett cave, and hauled out in dunes covered in marram grass, tree lupin and poroporo, right in front of Bill and Janice Wilson's place.

While mulling over that sequence of events I catch sight of an object in the surf, dark against the foam. Actually, there are two objects. One is clearly a canoe or kayak. Its occupant is working the paddles hard. They flash in the mid-afternoon sun. The other object is smaller and seemingly more manoeuvrable. It is surely not – how could it be? A sea lion?

I fumble for my binoculars. A kayak it most certainly is. Not one of those ocean-going craft with a long upturned prow but a shorter model with a blunt nose. The Lark had one of those. Come back in the summer, he said, and I'll show you something to do with sea lions.

Kayak and sea lion are tumbling about in the surf! From its size and dark colour I presume the animal is a male. It is a mesmerising scene. I walk out on to the sand bar to get more of a side-on view of the pair. With the tide probably just starting to make and no wind to speak of, the surf is fairly gentle. Nonetheless, the kayak leaps as it rides out into the waves and I can see the paddler jolted back by the foaming crests of the bigger waves. The sea lion is tracking the craft, although it disappears from view for periods. What sort of sport or performance is this? Man and wild beast surfing together.

The kayak catches a wave and is swiftly propelled towards the shore, with the sea lion either porpoising behind it or riding the same wave. At times the sea lion swims at an angle to the waves and encircles the craft much as a yappy dog might relate to its owner while on an outing to beach or park. When kayak and sea lion reach the slithering last line of surf they turn around and head back out through the breakers to beyond the surf zone, and the game resumes.

At times the kayak clips the top of a wave that is on the point of breaking, shadowed by a black form that is inclined to take the shortest route, driving straight through the middle of the wave.

The performance certainly makes up for shy spoonbills.

Not knowing whether to shout or wave or what, I decide that the paddler, if it is the Lark, will not be able to hear anything above the surf noise and that I might as well head back quickly to the car and try to catch up with him from the other side.

Half walking, half jogging, I shoot over the bar with hardly a care about what the tide is doing. The crossing takes about ten minutes. Nearing the park, I look back towards the mouth to see the kayak in the river. It is heading for the north bank and the shady patch that is the cave I now associate with the Lark and old Fred Tuckett, the pioneer surveyor.

Leaving my gumboots on, I take the car around to the other side of the river and make the short walk along the beach to find the Lark outside the cave and looking anything but a high country blade shearer. Sorting through a small pack, he is clad in a wet anorak, shorts and long-johns. His kayak, the purple Pirouette, is drawn up on the sand. He looks up, blue eyes shining, frizzy ginger hair darkened by the surf. His face is ruddy from the exertion of paddling and dusted by sea-salt crystals – or sweat.

'Now this is a turn-up for the books,' I say. 'I thought about hollering an Ahoy from the island side but I guess you wouldn't have heard anything.'

Seemingly unmoved about our meeting again, the Lark looks me up and down with a steady gaze.

'Gidday to you. Been a while. Did you get to that other island you were talking about last time we met? Down south. Ender-something.'

'Enderby. Certainly did, and the Auckland Island falcons send their greetings.'

'Oh, yeah?'

'They fly about in the rata forest, chasing parakeets.'

The Lark ponders this. He has slung the pack over his shoulder now, looking like he is going somewhere. His bare feet, wide and stocky, are half buried in the soft sand.

'Not like our rangeland birds, then,' he says.

I would have carried on discussing falcons but for the antics of a certain sea lion back there on the beach.

'Who's your surfie mate, then?'

'Ah, you saw him, did you? That's Brutus. Brute of a boy. Four years old, perhaps older. Not often we coincide here but when we do, I tell you, we have some fun and games. Don't know what happened to him today. He shot through all of a sudden. Might have been hungry. Or bored. Who knows?'

'He's not a tame one, then?"

'Hell, no. A Californian sea lion he is not. But you could call him an opportunist . . . he's got some go in him, no mistake. This time of year he's starting to look out for females, one in particular.

'Mum, by any chance?'

'Who?'

'You know, the mother sea lion. She's given birth here before. Researchers call her Mum.'

'Ah, yes. I know her. Keeps pretty much to herself. Don't blame her, with the likes of Brutus about.'

The Lark wanders over to his kayak and stuffs the pack into the rear compartment. He says he plans to ride the flood tide upstream to a campsite in the gorge.

'Need to grab a rest,' he says, 'and get out of this clammy gear. Tell you what, why don't you come back tomorrow and I'll introduce you to Brutus if he's here? Make it three o'clock. We'll have a brew. That a deal?'

'Look forward to it.'

The Lark slips into his kayak and paddles with purpose towards the lowering sun, which is casting a hazy golden glow over the river-run hills. Me, I take the tarseal river home, marvelling at how the interactions of man and beast can take the strangest turns. In New Zealand, which has few native mammals, you rarely encounter such stories.

FOUR

MOST OF THE WORLD'S MAMMALS are landlubbers. Of 4,000-odd species, fewer than three percent (some 116) are marine. The majority of these are whales and dolphins. The newest marine mammal is the North Pacific sea otter, which opted for a life at sea a mere two million years or so ago. It still has the front paws of a land carnivore, and no blubber yet, only fur, which it must keep in good condition if it is to survive. In contrast, the seal family have long since dispensed with bear-like paws in favour of flippers all round. The seals are divided into two broad groups – the 'crawlers' such as elephant seal and leopard seal, and the 'walkers', which describe the fur seals, sea lions and walruses. The crawlers are thought to have had an otter-like animal as an ancestor; the walkers probably descend from something akin to bears. But the debate about their origins rolls on through DNA analysis and much fossicking after fossils. No one knows for sure whether the seal family derives from two ancestors or one.

But why should a land mammal begin to live in the sea? I guess there are two main reasons – the 'pull' of food in abundance and the 'push' from land predators. When it comes to food supply, I have read of sheep in the Shetlands Islands of Scotland foraging for kelp in the intertidal zone, and I have seen pigs wandering the coral reefs of Tokelau, New Zealand's tropical 'Farthest North', in search of fish, sea slugs and small molluscs. Tokelau pigs can wade with their heads under water, and they even try swimming a bit, with their trotters scrambling for traction in the warm water. The subantarctic Auckland Island pigs, which have not had as long to adapt as their Tokelauan counterparts, feed on kelp and whatever else is available along the main island's rocky shores. If they survive long enough there, perhaps they will start swimming one day.

Not that the sea lions care a jot about all this. Nor the Lark probably. I have a few more questions for him about this Brutus character. Which is why I am driving south next day on the road to Taieri Mouth with my wetsuit in the back seat. Heavy overcast conditions hint at rain but only a landlubber would worry about that. There is a whiff of summer in the mild air temperatures.

A quick scan of the beach on the approach to the Mouth reveals no sign of life in the sullen surf so I carry on round the corner and check out the cave. Sure enough, the Lark is there, sitting on the sand but dressed more for the road than the ocean, a high country road at that. He is wearing a black singlet and floppy khaki shorts. Tanned shoulders, arms and legs, darkened by the cloudiness of the day, suggest an outdoor life. He reaches forward to lift the lid of the billy that is heating up water on a small gas burner. His kayak is parked nearby.

'No show, I'm afraid,' he says dully.

'No Brutus?'

'Gone fishing. And only he knows for how long. Take a pew for a brew.'

As I sit down on the sand the Lark throws a handful of tea leaves into the billy. They float unsurely on the top of the simmering water until he stirs them in then turns off the gas. For a few moments we are quiet and let the rumble of surf on the bar fill the space. From somewhere over by George McIntosh's place comes the staccato alarm call of a spur-winged plover. A harrier appears above the tall macrocarpas, trying its best to dodge the zig-zag attack of the plover. High country symbols, the pair of them. But then, so is the Lark. At least, he was until yesterday.

'This Brutus fellow,' I say, 'has he always been so approachable?'

'Too true. To me anyway. Guess most people would label him more frisky than approachable. He'll get back in the surf with me if he's reasonably fresh out of the water. But there's no moving him once he's been hunkered down in the dunes or on the sand for hours. Hope you don't take milk. Fresh out of cow.'

'No, I don't, but make mine weakish, thanks.'

The Lark tilts the billy towards an enamel mug. 'Black tea's not worth sneezing at if you can see the bottom.'

A cup of tea suits my purpose well. I put it to the Lark that because most people regard sea lions as being wild to the point of dangerous, they would rather take a running jump at the moon than join these animals in the surf. A few senseless citizens occasionally have a crack at them with a rifle or try running them over in an R.V.

'That's fear for you,' he says. 'Fear of being unable to control something. Bears and wolves produce the same reaction in North America. No bears or wolves here so we look for something else. To many people nature as raw as a sea lion is a frightening prospect. Thing is, you have to talk to your bête noire. Converse with it. Level with it. Come clean.'

'That's how it is with you and Brutus?'

'Pretty much. After a couple of years of doing this sort of thing, I reckon we're old hands at it now. I mean, the few sea lions I've seen here never seem to act in a hotheaded way. Look at the mother one. Very docile.'

'Is Brutus a potential mate for Mum, do you think?'

'Could be. Sea lions are not thick on the ground round here. Turn up in ones and twos. Towards Christmas I've noticed Brutus is more revved up. Gets itchy flippers. Could be he's thinking of migrating back to his birthplace for the breeding season, Auckland Islands is my guess.'

At the mention of the Auckland Islands the Lark pauses to see if I want to add anything. I let him continue.

'It was different last summer. He was more or less based round here and, yes, maybe Mum will be back to give birth this year.'

'Well, she'll break the two-year pupping pattern if she does,' I put in. 'But what makes you think Brutus is an Auckland Islander by birth?'

The Lark knocks back the last of his tea and stares at his bare feet. I am thinking there is more than a reasonable degree of webbing to those feet. Whether he has read my mind I cannot really say but his next comment floors me.

'Something selchie – '

'You mean the seal people thing? You're telling me you can communicate with Brutus?'

'Something like that. As I said, we level with each other. We have an understanding. It's hard to put it into words. Old Celtic tradition, you know.'

'Go on.'

'It's strong in the Hebrides. Islands like Lewis and the Outer Hebrides, too. My old grandpa was from there, and my father passed on stories about fisherfolk who somehow offended the gods and ended up living as seals. They're grey seals over there in Scotland. There were tales of seals talking and singing. Warning of disaster. Tales handed down in the half-light.'

'Are you telling me, Lark, that Brutus might be harbouring a human spirit?'

'Take out of it what you like.'

We fall into silence. There are some things beyond explaining, and this seems one of them. In another setting, the Strath

Taieri uplands, I have seen the Lark soaring freely with a falcon as if in communication with it. Now, here he is fraternising with a sea lion. It puts a new spin on the concept of extreme sports. I switch our conversation to firmer ground.

'Had any close calls kayaking in the surf?' I ask.

'Nah, it's all about going with the flow – the waves, bubbles, eddies. I've had a lot of practice going with the thermals hang-gliding. It's something of the sort here – surrendering to the elements, being spontaneous, letting go.'

The Lark has his eyes on the river now. Although its brown waters are still flowing strongly seaward, the river is swelling as the tide pushes a wedge of salt water underneath.

'Tide's on the make,' he says. 'I've got a ticket on this one. Gotta go. Due up country for a fencing job day after tomorrow so I'll be excusing myself.'

He packs up the little cooker and walks to the water's edge to rinse the cups.

'Spot you some other time,' he says, packing his things into the kayak. Then, 'But maybe not here.'

'Why's that?'

'Shouting myself a sojourn out west. The big country. Feel like a sea change, a break from the farm labouring racket. Coming up sixty, you know.' He slips into the cockpit of his kayak and pushes off from the sandy bank. 'Think I'll head up past Glenorchy and see what I can see. Head of the Wakatip. Real mountains.'

He grimaces momentarily, perhaps at the thought of all the walking. His eyes narrow. There is a glint in them that puts me in mind of the twinkle in a kea's eye. He is paddling now and pulling away, and I have no doubt he will find mountains to climb where he can reverse gravity. The Lark is like that.

Me, I'll stay coasting a while.

Ongoings

MUM HAD HER FOURTH PUP that summer, upriver by Bill Wilson's house. A boy it was, and the scientists named him Bill. I saw Bill a couple of days after he was born. Mum was guarding him on a flat sandy piece of ground at the foot of a set of low cliffs, above which houses gaze out over the estuary. He seemed a little bolder than his three sisters at the same age. You have to hand it to Mum – four pups in seven years, three of them precious females, and all guided back safely to Victory Beach on Otago Peninsula.

I met young Bill in the autumn on a visit to Papanui Inlet, a teardrop of the sea couched behind Victory Beach. Four months old, the youngster was splashing about in a tidal pool at the edge of the inlet, more than a kilometre from the beach and his nursery in the pines. I was hoping to catch up with Bill and his mother but hardly expected to find him alone so far from the usual stamping ground of sea lions. As I approached he looked up with a concerned expression, as if caught out, a naughty boy for straying so far from camp. How would he react? Would he wander over to say hello or would he bolt for cover? He did the latter, at a clattering gallop, too. He made for the grassy bank marking the edge of the inlet and scrambled up it, flippers flailing. With liquid eyes, large and dark and knowing, he watched from behind some tussocks as I moved slowly past.

Out at the beach I encountered a sea lion sleepy hollow – three males slumbering in the dunes and one nodding off at the edge of the apron of sand. None stirred as I walked past them. Into the pines I plunged, not hopeful of bumping into Mum. If her pup was out exploring the inlet, chances are she would be at sea. At that moment clouds dimmed the sun, making the interior of the plantation a sombre place. I did a zig-zag through the trees, following dark avenues and the crests of several dunes, but found nothing but piles of sea lion droppings lying desiccated on the thick layer of pine needles.

Emerging from the plantation farther along the beach, I stopped for a drink at the top of the high foredune. Before me lay the sea in panorama, now dappled with sunlight. I perched myself on a clump of marram. No city in the world I know of encompasses beaches as secluded as Victory Beach and its neighbours. Victory, three kilometres long, is magnificent in its isolation. You can sit at a place like this, far from tarseal, traffic lights and office towers, and let your imagination wander. Only the rust-gnarled flywheel of the steamship *Victory*, half exposed in the surf zone, seeks to direct it – in this case to the foolhardiness of those who take the sea for granted.

Beyond the wreck, the sea this day is a blue tapestry, woven with waves. It has texture. It is an exquisite fabric. Blues of many shades shimmer with silver sequins. You are drawn to fondle it with your thoughts and wonder at its attraction, which is quite different from the pull of the mountains. The sea invites introspection, a journey inward and with feeling – the Lark's 'ocean emotion'. Mountains, on the other hand, invite a response that is more outgoing – outgoing to the point of rapture. Whereas you can get the measure of mountains, or at least think you can, the sea is never as revealing, never as submitting. It guards its secrets well.

And like all surf beaches, this is a resonant place. The surf conveys an awesome energy, each breaker a drum-roll and clash of cymbals announcing the sea's underlying power and restlessness, born of distant storms interacting with currents, oceanic fronts, water masses and finally the sweep of the tide up the coast. It is as if the breakers are gallant messengers, trailing resplendent white capes and bearing stories passed on at sea from wave to wave. Rocky shores tend to receive the stories noisily; beaches hear them in a whisper.

Suddenly she is there, a short distance along the beach. A silvery sea bear, slumped on the sand and still wet – a story and a half. Now she raises herself on weary flippers and waddles a few more metres towards the pines, leaving a trail of half-moons in the sand. By the time I climb down to the beach she is heading up a beaten pathway to the plantation, bawling out at intervals, clearly trumpeting her return to her pup. I follow her into the forest.

'Looking for your pup, are you? Well, boys will be boys, you know. Bill's away exploring the inlet.'

Mum keeps moving on steadily through a lane of trees, calling like a steer, and pausing to listen for any response. There is none. She is almost right through to the other side of the plantation before she decides that Bill is nowhere in the vicinity and the best thing to do is take a rest. She picks a flattish spot and begins flicking pine needles across her back, more out of habit and for comfort than because she needs protection from the sun.

Mum, the matriarch, is home.

I sit with her for about 15 minutes, hoping I might see Bill return. But he does not show. Ignoring me, Mum is soon asleep and snoring softly.

'Mum', the matriarch of Otago sea lions in modern times, on Victory Beach, Otago Peninsula.

PHOTO: NEVILLE PEAT

Acknowledgements

For information, inspiration and hospitality I am most grateful to Taieri Mouth identities George McIntosh and Martin Palmer and their wives, Juliet and Barbara. Bill Wilson also made me welcome and Graham Fraser kindly gave me a ride to the island in his fishing boat.

Advice about sea lions came from Nick Gales, Chris Lalas, Simon Childerhouse, Martin Cawthorn, Shaun McConkey, Sonja Heinrik and Gail Dickie. I take responsibility for embellishments contained in the narrative accounts. I thank Chris Lalas especially for letting me join him on field trips on Otago Peninsula. Ian Smith, Jill Hamel and Philip Houghton provided archaeological information.

For the expedition to the Auckland Islands I thank scientists Nick Gales and Simon Childerhouse, skipper Lance Shaw and his crew. Kayaking advice was kindly provided by Chris Wright and Andy Beecroft.

For her skilful editing I thank Emma Neale. I am also grateful to Oxford University Press for permission to reproduce the James K. Baxter poems, published in Baxter's *Collected Poems*, 1980.